COMBAT AIRCRAFT

139 DORNIER Do 217 UNITS
OF WORLD WAR 2

SERIES EDITOR TONY HOLMES

139

COMBAT AIRCRAFT

Chris Goss

DORNIER Do 217 UNITS OF WORLD WAR 2

OSPREY
PUBLISHING

OSPREY PUBLISHING
Bloomsbury Publishing Plc

Kemp House, Chawley Park, Cumnor Hill, Oxford OX2 9PH, UK
29 Earlsfort Terrace, Dublin 2, Ireland
1385 Broadway, 5th Floor, New York, NY 10018, USA
Email: info@ospreypublishing.com
www.ospreypublishing.com

OSPREY is a trademark of Osprey Publishing Ltd

First published in Great Britain in 2021

Print ISBN: 978 1 4728 4617 4
ePub: 978 1 4728 4618 1
ePDF: 978 1 4728 4615 0
XML: 978 1 4728 4616 7

Edited by Tony Holmes
Cover artwork by Mark Postlethwaite
Aircraft profiles by Janusz Światłoń
Index by Sandra Shotter
Originated by PDQ Digital Media Solutions, UK
Printed and bound in Great Britain

22 23 24 25 26   10 9 8 7 6 5 4 3 2

The Woodland Trust

Osprey Publishing supports the Woodland Trust, the UK's leading woodland
conservation charity.

www.ospreypublishing.com

To find out more about our authors and books visit our website. Here you
will find extracts, author interviews, details of forthcoming events and the
option to sign-up for our newsletter.

Front Cover

At 1137 hrs on 16 December 1942,
Do 217E-4 Wk-Nr 5581 U5+KL of 3./KG 2
took off from Gilze-Rijen airfield, in the
Netherlands, to undertake a 'Pirate' attack
on targets in Hampshire and Dorset. It was
crewed by Oberleutnant Karl von
Manowarda (pilot), Feldwebel Heinrich
Kaiser (observer), Feldwebel Ernst Fröhlich
(radio operator) and Oberfeldwebel Heinrich
Bühr (flight engineer). At 1333 hrs the
Do 217 emerged from cloud over Wareham,
in Dorset, and, from an altitude of 450 m,
dropped four 500 kg bombs, before
disappearing back into cloud. Five houses
were destroyed, 80 damaged, a gasometer
set on fire and telephone lines cut. Fourteen
people were also injured, but none killed.
The aircraft is depicted here in the low-
visibility scheme applied to a handful of
Do 217s in the West, the camouflage
proving well suited to daylight raids when
crews relied on cloud and bad weather for
cover. Wk-Nr 5581, flown by the same pilot,
would be damaged in combat with a
Beaufighter of No 29 Sqn on 4 January
1943. Still coded U5+KL, the bomber was
eventually lost flying with 1./KG 2 during an
attack on London on the night of 3 March
1943 – Oberfeldwebel Walter Birkner and
his crew were all reported missing, believed
killed (Cover artwork by Mark Postlethwaite)

PREVIOUS PAGES

Do 217E-4 Wk-Nr 4279 F8+CN of
5./KG 40 in night camouflage typical of this
unit. On 24 July 1942, this aircraft was shot
down near Holbeach, in south Lincolnshire,
by a Beaufighter from No 409 Sqn and a
Typhoon from No 486 Sqn. Oberleutnant
Heinrich Viess and his three crew bailed out
and were captured. It is believed that Wk-Nr
4279 was the first E-4 to crash on
British soil

All photographs in this volume are from the
author's collection

Acknowledgements

The author would like to thank Nick Beale,
Theo Boiten, Gianandrea Bussi, Steven
Coates, Robert Forsyth, Marcel van Heikop,
Tim Oliver, Frank Olynyk, Bernd Rauchbach,
Andy Saunders, Chris Simmons, Günther
Steudel, Dave Wadman, Dave Williams and
Georg Wolff for their assistance with the
compilation of this volume.

CONTENTS

DESIGN, DEVELOPMENT AND INTO ACTION

At the end of September 1938, the idea of a modernised Dornier Do 17 was first raised by the Luftwaffe. Full production of the Junkers Ju 88 had yet to be achieved, while much effort was now going into the Heinkel He 177 long-range heavy bomber programme. The larger Dornier was designed in response to Specification 1323, released at the beginning of 1938, which called for a twin-engined bomber capable of long-range missions. The aircraft was to be powered by the highly promising Daimler-Benz DB 601B engine. Basing its new bomber on the tried and tested Do 17, Dornier proposed an aircraft with a wider cockpit and a larger bomb-bay capable of carrying 1500 kg of bombs. Compared to the Do 17M (which was just entering production in 1938), the Specification 1323 design had a wingspan that was a metre larger – the wings also boasted dive brakes.

Although the new aircraft was designed principally as a level bomber, it was anticipated that it could also be used in the maritime attack role and as a heavy fighter. The specification, therefore, had the aircraft fitted with floats, having a range of 1500 km and a solid nose with four fixed guns. However, arguments between the Luftwaffe and Kriegsmarine as to whether the aircraft should be land-based or not, and the emergence of

The fourth Do 217 prototype, V4 Wk-Nr 690 is seen here at Friedrichshafen. Allotted the code CN+HL, the aircraft was powered by Jumo 211A-1 and then B-1 engines. It is fitted with an MG 15 machine gun in the nose

other aircraft types, meant that development of a naval version, called the 'See Stuka', soon ceased, while work on the more conventional machine continued.

On 4 October 1938, the first prototype Do 217 V1 Wk-Nr 687, powered by DB 601A engines, completed its maiden flight. Exactly a week later the aircraft crashed at Tettnang, northeast of Dornier's headquarters at Friedrichshafen, in southern Germany, killing pilot Diplom Ingenieur Rolf Köppe and flight engineer Egon Bausenhart. Undeterred, the company had the first development aircraft, Do 217 V2 Wk-Nr 688, which was identical to the V1 but with addition of a tail dive brake, ready to fly less than a month later. Between October 1938 and July 1940, a total of ten prototypes were flown, with each aircraft differing in its designed role (reconnaissance and bomber) and powerplants up to the V8. From then on, the majority of Do 217s would be fitted with BMW 801 radial engines.

At the same time, several other variants were being considered. Six Do 217A-0s (Wk-Nr 2701 to 2706) were produced, fitted with two Rb 50/30 cameras in the cockpit and an Rb 20/30 camera in the fuselage and powered, initially, by DB 601A or B engines. Manned by a crew of three, these aircraft were assigned to Oberst Theodor Rowehl's clandestine 1./*Aufklärungsgruppe Oberbefehlshaber der Luftwaffe* at the start of January 1940, although their time in service with this unit would be short. Later flown by such units as 10./*Kampfgeschwader* (KG) 2 and IV./KG 40 as aircrew trainers, the last recorded mention of a Do 217A-0 serving with a frontline unit came on 30 March 1942 when Wk-Nr 2703 was apparently lost in an accident near Osnabrück while flying with 10./KG 2, killing Leutnant Gerold Buss and two crew. A further Do 217A-0 (Wk-Nr 2706) survived to serve with *Flugzeugführerschule* (C) 5 at Neubrandenburg in January 1943.

Nine Do 217C-0s (Wk-Nr 2710 to 2718), powered by Jumo 211B or DB 601A engines, were completed as bombers but the only mention of any of these aircraft came after Wk Nr 2710 was lost in an accident while flying with the *Erprobungsstaffel der Luftwaffe* at Rechlin on 4 July 1941, killing test pilot Adolf Ostermaier and two crew.

However, both the A- and C-variants were secondary to what would become the first Do 217 to enter full operational service, the Do 217E.

Following heavy losses suffered by Do 17 units over Poland, France and during the Battle of Britain, priority was given to bomber production, and in particular the next generation of Dornier bombers. The Do 217C would now form the basis for the E-1, powered by BMW 801MA-1 engines. The prototype was first flown on 1 October 1940, the same month that Do 17 production ceased. Surprisingly, the aircraft enjoyed a relatively problem-free test programme, and by the end of March 1941, 37 Do 217E-1s had

The Do 217A-0, of which just six were produced, was fitted with cameras and assigned to 1./*Aufklärungsgruppe Oberbefehlshaber der Luftwaffe* from January 1940 for clandestine missions. Powered by DB 601 engines and carrying a crew of three, the A-0s were soon assigned transport or training roles with other units. This aircraft is believed to have been painted grey overall, and it was marked with the code T5 on the fuselage

been built and test flown. A total of 94 would be constructed before production switched to the Do 217E-2, with 185 examples being completed. The principle difference between the two types centred on armament, with the E-1 bomber being fitted with up to five 7.92 mm MG 15 machine guns for defence and a fixed forward-firing 20 mm MG 151 autocannon for low-level attacks. The E-2 dive-bomber relied on three MG 15s and two 13 mm MG 131 machine guns (one of which was fitted in a rear-firing dorsal turret), plus the fixed MG 151/20.

Testing continued with *Erprobungsstaffel der Luftwaffe* at Rechlin from late 1940 through to eventual completion in March 1942. Aircraft had, however, started to reach the frontline from the spring of 1941 when Major Kurt Rohde's II./KG 2 began to replace its Do 17Zs with Do 217E-1s. One of the first pilots to make the switch was Oberfeldwebel Hans Wolff of 6./KG 2, who, by the end of the Battle of Britain, was an experienced NCO. Commissioned as an Oberleutnant at the start of November 1940, Wolff was amongst a number of personnel from the *Staffel* sent to Oberpfaffenhofen on 18 January 1941 for familiarisation on the Do 217. He did not return to 6./KG 2 at Saint-Léger, in the Pas-de-Calais, until 24 February 1941, and he would continue flying Do 17s from there until May 1941.

By then most of II./KG 2 had returned to Achmer, in Germany, the *Gruppe* having been transferred home in March–April 1941. It would be followed by Oberstleutnant Heinrich Conrady's III./KG 2 in September 1941 and by Major Robert-Heinrich von Goddeck's I./KG 2 two months later after both *Gruppe* had carried out operations with the Do 17 over the Soviet Union.

Another early convert to the Do 217 was Oberstleutnant Dr Georg Pasewaldt's II./KG 40, which began forming in May 1941 as a maritime bomber unit flying the He 111. The *Gruppe* also received examples of the new Dornier bomber, with 4./KG 40 being the first to convert to the Do 217 from June 1941 onwards. Initially, the *Staffel* came under I./KG 40 control, but when it was expanded to *Gruppe* strength as II./KG 40, Hauptmann Wendt Freiherr von Schlippenbach assumed control after Oberstleutnant Dr Pasewaldt was given command of KG 40.

The first Do 217-equipped unit to suffer any kind of loss was 6./KG 2 on 22 February 1941 when the E-1 flown by Leutnant Valentin Wagner suffered an engine failure, while on 11 April Do 217E-1 Wk-Nr 1006, coded F8+HP, of 6./KG 40 also received damage in a minor accident. Within weeks of this incident occurring, the new Dornier bomber would make its combat debut.

Conversion training complete, II./KG 2 moved to Evreux, in France, at the start of July 1941, and duly flew its first mission, against the RAF airfield at Pembrey, in Wales, on the night of 5-6 July 1941. However, it

Dornier engineers working on a Do 217E-2 that has the last two digits of the Werknummer – 52 – on the nose. This could indicate that the aircraft is Wk-Nr 1152, which was damaged in an accident at Amsterdam-Schiphol while being flown by II./KG 2. In the background is Do 217 V8 Wk-Nr 2708 CO+JL, which first flew on 21 March 1940 and was the test aircraft for the BMW 801 engines as the prototype Do 217E-1

was not long before the first combat loss came when, during a series of daylight attacks on shipping on 14 July, the Do 217E-1 of 5./KG 2 flown by Feldwebel Kurt Bergmann reported being under attack by fighters near Land's End at 1605 hrs and failed to return. At around the same time, Hurricane pilots Flt Lt Henryk Szczęsny and Sgt Stanisław Brzeski of No 317 Sqn reported shooting down what they thought was a Ju 88 south of Tenby. Their combat report read as follows;

'Blue Section took off from Fairwood Common to patrol convoy ten miles south of Worms Head. At 1620 hrs, when in position, received no vector. While turning to port in steep bank at 600-1,000 ft, Blue 1 sighted Ju 88 [sic] approaching convoy from north to south 500 yards away and at sea-level. Blue 1 informed Blue 2 and ordered him to follow, giving boost. Blue 1 dived head on and a little to starboard towards enemy aircraft, turning sharply to port and delivering two two-second bursts at 200 yards on enemy aircraft port beam on same level. Enemy aircraft remained on same course and Blue 1 followed, continuing to turn to port. Meanwhile, Blue 2 cut across to port and also delivered beam attack at 250 yards, firing continuous bursts. Enemy aircraft jettisoned bombs 150 yards before convoy and hopped over first ship, causing Blue 1 to hold his fire. As enemy aircraft rose over second ship, Blue 1 opened fire at 250 yards, closing to 50 yards. They flew beside enemy aircraft as it lost speed from 220-120 mph at sea-level. The tail touched the water twice and enemy aircraft hit the water with starboard wing and sank, tail disappearing.'

This Do 217E-1 is carrying two SC 500 500 kg bombs ahead of two SC 250 250 kg weapons in its bomb-bay. The E-model could in fact be loaded with up to four 500 kg bombs

The location, time and the fact that no other German aircraft were lost this day would indicate that the two Polish pilots had accounted for the first Do 217 to be downed in combat. II./KG 40 suffered its first loss on the night of 9 August when Oberleutnant Kurt Müller of *Stab* II./KG 40 failed to return from an unspecified mission.

By then the bomber offensive was far less intense than it had been a year earlier, with the Luftwaffe resorting to using smaller numbers of aircraft both by night or in poor weather during the hours of daylight. With only a relative handful of the new Do 217s in the frontline, the Dornier was still an unfamiliar aircraft to the RAF. For example, on 16 July, Plt Off Bob Masters of Spitfire-equipped No 234 Sqn claimed to have shot down a 'dark camouflaged Do 215' 20 miles south of Portland at 1100 hrs when in fact he had intercepted the Do 217E-1 of 4./KG 2 flown by Leutnant Anton Winners, who had been briefed to attack Gloucester. Winners' last radio message corresponds with the time that the combat took place. Losing Winners hit KG 2 hard, for he had completed more than 100 operational flights and was soon expected to receive the *Ritterkreuz*.

Then, on 21 August, Leutnant Hans Röpke from 6./KG 40 failed to return from a sortie to the east coast of England, his aircraft probably being shot down by Plt Off Hugh 'Johnny' Johnstone of No 257 Sqn. The Hurricane pilot reported downing a Do 17 15 miles east of Lowestoft while on a convoy patrol, his fighter being damaged by return fire. Finally, on the evening of 7 September, Flg Off Robert 'Moose' Fumerton of Beaufighter-equipped No 406 Sqn damaged what he thought was an He 111 during an attack on Newcastle. It was more likely that he mortally damaged the Do 217E-1 of 4./KG 40 flown by Feldwebel Walter Nomming, which subsequently crashed into the North Sea northwest of Texel on its return flight.

The first confirmed evidence of the new bomber came on the night of 2 October, although the RAF initially recorded the aircraft as a Do 17 despite having captured three of its crew. Feldwebel Fritz Menzel from Do 217E-2-equipped 5./KG 2 took off from Amsterdam-Schiphol at 2000 hrs to attack Newcastle, and at 2120 hrs, radio operator Feldwebel Horst Schleussner spotted what he thought was a Ju 88. The aircraft was in fact a Beaufighter of No 406 Sqn flown by Wg Cdr Douglas 'Zulu' Morris, with Sgt Archie Rix as his radar operator. They would claim two victories during the course of the mission, although the first aircraft they engaged at 2050 hrs – a He 111H-6 of 9./KG 40, flown by Leutnant Walter Leitenberger – managed to limp back to its base at Soesterberg, in the Netherlands, with damage.

Wg Cdr Morris' combat report provided the following details for the second encounter;

'After reloading the cannon, the Beaufighter returned to GCI [Ground-Control Intercept] and at 2115 hrs made contact with a Do 17 approaching Tynemouth from the east. Closing to 2500 ft on AI [Air Intercept radar], our aircraft made a three-quarter circle to port and pursued the enemy as he turned south. First burst at 100 yards was returned; a second was followed by a terrific explosion, the enemy disappeared and the Beaufighter flew through the flash and cloud of sparks. Four apparent parachutes and a mark on the surface were seen below about three miles east of Tynemouth. With port glycol tank punctured, Wg Cdr Morris landed at Acklington at 2143 hrs.'

The surviving German crewmen reported being attacked twice from the rear starboard quarter, the radio operator managing to return fire from the top turret. However, one of the rudders was damaged in the engagement and flight engineer Unteroffizier Arno Herold was badly wounded. The bomber quickly fell away in a spiral dive and then exploded, throwing out all four crew. Although Menzel subsequently drowned, the remaining crew were picked up by a trawler eight miles east-northeast of Tynemouth. Interrogation of the two unwounded crew revealed that they had converted to the Do 217 at Bramsche in May–June 1941 and, following six weeks of training, had initially moved to Evreux before transferring to Schiphol at the end of September.

The RAF was now fully aware of the Do 217, and by mid-October 1941 KG 2 had lost ten aircraft on operations, four of them as a direct result of enemy action, while II./KG 40 had lost three, with two definitely shot down by the RAF. So far, all downed aircraft had crashed into the sea, and the RAF would have to wait until 12 October to see the new type up close. Oberleutnant Günther Dolenga of 5./KG 2 described the fate that befell he and his crew that night;

'On my last flight I had orders to attack shipping west of the Scilly Isles, in the Irish Sea and in the Bristol Channel. The RAF's No. 80 [Signals] Wing hunted my crew over Britain using Meacon beacons,

Do 217E-2 Wk-Nr 1144 RH+ER was lost in action on 22 March 1943 with 5./KG 2 (by which point the bomber was coded U5+IN) when it was shot down attacking Hartlepool, in County Durham. The aircraft was possibly shot down by Flg Off Robert Sargent of No 219 Sqn, Wk-Nr 1144 crashing into the sea off Cullercoats, then in Northumberland, and killing Feldwebel Rudolf Wenkel and his crew

The first Do 217 to be captured almost intact was E-1 Wk-Nr 5069 U5+DN of 5./KG 2 on 12 October. Confused by spoof radio beacons, Oberleutnant Günther Dolenga and his crew became lost and thought they were 30 kilometres northwest of Le Havre when, in fact, they were over East Sussex. The pilot duly force-landed in Jury's Gap Sewer near Rye. Note the absence of a turret at the rear of the cockpit, which confirms this is an E-1 variant

which meant I was walking into a trap. That's not quite right – I was in the trap, and upon realising it, I turned southwards after receiving a bearing from Evreux. At this moment my fuel was running low due to a block in the fuel line. At first I thought it was damage caused by a nightfighter, so I decided to make a crash-landing on the shore because I had a good indication that I couldn't reach the French coast. Today, I am convinced that this decision was better than a crash-landing at sea, and getting a wooden coat [coffin]!'

Pushed off track by high winds, the crew was further confused by No 80 Wing's Meacon beacons at Templecombe, in Somerset, and Newbury, in Berkshire, which led Dolenga to believe he was over France – RAF controllers at Templecombe had pretended to be the German navigation beacon at Paimpol, in Brittany. 'Meaconing' is best described as the interception and rebroadcasting of enemy navigation signals, giving inaccurate bearings so as to confuse navigators on board German bombers. As a result of the 'Meaconing', and having crossed southern England from north Devon to East Sussex, the German crew eventually crash-landed at Broomhill, near Rye in East Sussex. They had only realised where they were when one of the crew spotted a soldier in a British steel helmet. Rushing back to the crashed bomber, they tried to destroy the Do 217 but failed, thus handing the RAF a complete, if not bent, Do 217E-1.

Furthermore, Dolenga was an experienced pilot, having flown in Poland, the Battle of Britain, the Blitz and in Greece. He was expected to assume command of 5./KG 2 from Oberleutnant Alfred Kindler, who had only recently taken control of the *Staffel* following the grounding of Hauptmann Ulrich Linnemann through illness. Kindler (who would subsequently receive the *Ritterkreuz* after his capture in July 1942) took over 6./KG 2 on 20 October 1941 following the death in an accident of *Ritterkreuz* holder Hauptmann Gerhard Czernik, whose Do 217E-2 suffered an engine failure and crashed northeast of Schiphol.

The relative intactness of Dolenga's aircraft gave the Royal Aircraft Establishment (RAE) at Farnborough, in Hampshire, ample time to carry out a full technical assessment, including producing detailed reports on its structure, knife edge cutters, de-icing equipment, electrical dive-bombing gear, armour plating and bombing installation. It also meant RAE technical personnel could compile reports that informed

RAF nightfighter crews about what they were now up against, describing the aircraft as follows;

'The Do 217 is a twin-engined, high wing medium bomber and general reconnaissance aircraft carrying a crew of four. As in the Do 17 and Ju 88, the crew are all placed together in a cabin entirely forward of the wing leading edge. The machine has a span of 62 ft 5 in and is entirely metal covered. The tailplane is of variable incidence and carries twin rudders, and provision is made for the installation of umbrella-style tail dive brakes, which were not present in the machine examined. The engines are of the BMW 801A double row 14 cylinder radial direct injection type and are mounted in nacelles underslung from the wing.

'The structure of the aeroplane is divided into several main assembly units – the main wing and fuselage centre section, carrying the engines, undercarriage and main fuel tanks; the outer wings; the fore part of the fuselage; the rear fuselage; the tail unit. Those sub-assemblies are built up as separate units and are presumably interchangeable with their counterparts. At each main joint, the sub-assemblies are bolted together and the control rods, electric cables and hydraulic pipelines are connected in a manner suited to ready dismantling for repair and maintenance work. This machine is remarkable for its diversity of electrical equipment, hydraulic systems being used only for the brakes and propeller pitch controls.'

Dolenga's E-1, Wk-Nr 5069 coded U5+DN, would be the first of many Do 217s to crash on British soil over the next two-and-a-half years.

The final ten weeks of 1941 would be much quieter for KG 2 and II./KG 40. Three aircraft of II./KG 2 returned damaged by flak and nightfighters during this period, while the *Gruppe's* only combat loss occurred on 1 November when Leutnant Bruno Adler from 4./KG 2 was shot down off Watchet, in Somerset, by a Beaufighter from No 307 Sqn flown by Sgt Bolesław Turzański during an attack on Liverpool. The Polish pilot correctly claimed two Do 217s, rather than Do 17s, that night, the second aircraft probably being the E-2 of 5./KG 2 that returned with three wounded crew, one of whom was observer Leutnant Helmut Petraschke.

As for Soesterberg-based II./KG 40, it continued to predominantly attack coastal targets and shipping in the North Sea. On 27 October, the Do 217E-2 flown by Leutnant Helmut Rösch of 5./KG 40 was lost while attacking convoy FN537, consisting of ten ships without escort, which had sailed from Southend, in Essex, the previous day bound for Methil, on the east coast of Scotland. A second aircraft from 4./KG 40 returned

Do 217s encountered by RAF fighter pilots in the skies over Britain during the summer and autumn of 1941 were initially misidentified as Do 17s, Do 215s and even Ju 88s. However, following the crash-landing of the intact example in East Sussex, the Air Ministry was subsequently able to produce this detailed recognition/identification poster to educate RAF pilots and anti-aircraft gunners

with a wounded flight engineer. At around 1430 hrs that day, Sgt John Slaney, flying a Hurricane from No 257 Sqn, claimed a Do 217 destroyed off Happisburgh, in Norfolk. Sqn Ldr Charles Green, commanding officer (CO) of Spitfire-equipped No 266 Sqn, assisted by Sgt Eric Dicks-Sherwood, shot down another Do 217 over the convoy at 1800 hrs, their target, identified again as a Do 17Z, crashing ten miles off Happisburgh Lighthouse.

Leutnant Gerhard Blaschke of 5./KG 2 reportedly took off from Evreux at 1359 hrs that afternoon on an armed reconnaissance mission off the east coast of England, landing at Schiphol two-and-a-half hours later after an uneventful mission. It would appear, therefore, that II./KG 40 was responsible for sinking the 4545-ton SS *Antiope* and the Dutch-registered 2662-ton *Friesland* eight miles north-northwest of Cromer, in Norfolk.

The *Gruppe*'s last operational loss of the year came on 12 November. Oberleutnant Herwig Schmid of 4./KG 40 took off from Soesterberg at 0848 hrs on an armed reconnaissance mission over the North Sea coast, and at 1047 hrs he reported attacking a ship off Lowestoft, in Suffolk, after which nothing more was heard from him. It is believed that he attacked the Royal Navy trawlers HMT *Francolin*, commanded by Lt J L Dinwoodie, and HMT *Commander Holbrook*, commanded by Chief A S V Jones, off Happisburgh. *Francolin* was sunk with the loss of one crewman, while the Do 217, again misidentified as a Do 17, was either hit by light anti-aircraft fire or collided with the mast of the 322-ton trawler and crashed into the sea two miles off Happisburgh Lighthouse with the loss of all four crew.

So ended the first five months of operations for the Do 217. Amongst the pilots to see combat in the aircraft during this period was Oberleutnant Josef Steudel of 8./KG 2, who would have a long association with both the Do 17 and Do 217. He wrote of the new bomber;

'A positive expectant spirit accompanied our training on the Do 217. This aircraft was, at that time, the Luftwaffe's most modern bomber. Its appearance was very similar to the Do 17, but the most apparent difference was that it was no longer as sleek as the Do 17. It had a more voluminous fuselage and could carry 2000 kg [of ordnance], twice the load of the Do 17. The Do 217 was also very similar in its manoeuvrability. It was much heavier and therefore less agile, and yet it was very responsive and easy to fly. Still, it must be said that in July 1941, it was still not ready to be deployed to the Front. Many inadequacies were still to be discovered, and it required constant changes, improvements and refitting. In all of the years of the war, we were hardly ever at full strength, and escalating losses were a major cause of this.'

The inadequacies of the Do 217 would become increasingly obvious as more examples reached the frontline.

Do 217E-2 Wk-Nr 1145 RH+ES awaits delivery to a frontline unit after completion by Dornier. Note the last two digits of the Werknummer within the fuselage cross. This aircraft, which was later upgraded into an E-4, suffered extensive damage at Vannes on 11 August 1943 when a tyre burst on landing. By then the bomber was coded U5+ZN and assigned to 5./KG 2. Pilot Unteroffizier Ulrich Bachmann and crew were uninjured in the incident

CHAPTER TWO

NEED FOR CHANGE

By 5 January 1942, III./KG 2, now commanded by Major Gerhard Klostermann, had arrived at Schiphol after converting to the Do 217 at Achmer. It joined Major Robert-Heinrich von Groddeck's I./KG 2, Hauptmann Walter Bradel's II./KG 2 and Hauptmann Wendt Freiherr von Schlippenbach's II./KG 40 at Soesterberg, all four *Gruppen* then moving to other bases temporarily as dictated by the location of targets they were attacking. Although the missions being flown were the same as they had been the previous year, Do 217 crews now faced a new threat to their survival, as Oberleutnant Josef Steudel of 8./KG 2 explained;

'The war had us again. Our targets were the familiar harbour towns on the east, south and west coasts, industrial centres in the Midlands and also convoys. Part of the job was mining the Channel and the mouth of the Thames. What was unfamiliar was the new British defence. Radar-guided nightfighters were making our life increasingly difficult, and the new technology was seeing rapid improvements and we would suffer severe losses. "Missing in Action" became a standard turn of phrase. During our missions with the Do 17, we could afford to keep flying on a predetermined course. Now, anyone who continued flying in this manner was in grave danger of being shot down by nightfighters.'

Due to the increasing effectiveness of British defences, the Do 217E needed to be improved. The E-3 (an upgraded E-1) and E-4 (based on the

This sinister-looking Do 217E-2/4 was photographed during operations at dusk. Close examination of the tail reveals the code F8+IM, which would indicate an aircraft from 4./KG 40. On 27 October 1941, Do 217E-2 Wk-Nr 1126 force-landed at Quakenbrück after being damaged in combat with fighters from No 257 Sqn. The following day, E-2 Wk-Nr 5326 from 5./KG 40 was shot down off Cromer by No 266 Sqn

E-2) had additional armour protection and changes to defensive weapons and their calibre.

Those crews that had recently arrived at Schiphol after conversion training were soon in action. For example, Oberleutnant Rudolf Häusner and his crew flew their first mission in a Do 217 on 13 January when they undertook an armed reconnaissance operation over the North Sea. Two days later, they targeted Whitby, in Yorkshire, followed by an attack on a convoy off Withernsea on 22 January. The crew of Oberfeldwebel Georg Brendebach targeted Liverpool on 10 January (Brendebach's 63rd mission of the war) and dropped mines in the Thames Estuary the following night, but then did not fly again until 3 March.

Do 217 losses were initially light, with the first occurring in the early hours of 11 January 1942. Oberfeldwebel Paul Wolf's bomber from 5./KG 40 was one of 16 aircraft briefed to attack Merseyside, and although the crew managed to drop their bombs without difficulty, when they turned for home they were intercepted by a Beaufighter of No 456 Sqn flown by Sqn Ldr John Hamilton, with Plt Off Dan Norris-Smith as his radar operator. The nightfighter crew subsequently reported;

'At 0055 hrs given vector onto raid by Hack Green GCI. Flying at 22,000 ft, contacted enemy aircraft crossing at right angles at a height of 12,000 ft. Operator gave 90-degree turn and second contact made. Visual then obtained at 150 yards astern and 50 ft below. Pilot fired two bursts and enemy aircraft (Do 217) shot down in flames.'

The Beaufighter had been spotted just before its attack, but Wolf took no evasive action. A second attack set the starboard engine on fire and the crew bailed out, the bomber crashing southwest of Nuneaton, in Warwickshire.

Losses for the remainder of January were light. Feldwebel Joachim Lehnis and his crew from 8./KG 2 were lost during the evening of the 15th while engaged on yet another armed reconnaissance along the east coast of England. It is possible that the bomber attacked and damaged SS *Empire Bay* off Middlesbrough, only to then head inland, where the Do 217E-2 collided with a barrage balloon cable which severed nine feet off one of its wings. The aircraft crashed onto railway lines at Clay Lane, in South Bank, Middlesbrough, shortly thereafter, killing all four crew. That same night, 6./KG 40 lost Leutnant Karl Dern and his crew, who radioed that they had lost an engine and were returning to base – they never arrived. Finally, in what proved to be a black day for the Do 217 force, Oberfeldwebel Ludwig Ehle and his crew were killed taking off from Soesterberg. These were the last two losses for II./KG 40 in January, but not so for KG 2.

On the 17th, Feldwebel Otto Thomas of 8./KG 2 was shot down attacking a convoy off Clacton-on-Sea, on the Essex coast, by gunners on board HMS *Walpole* and a Havoc flown by Plt Off Hugh Norsworthy of No 85 Sqn. The final two losses of the month were on the night of 21 January, again off the east coast of England. Oberleutnant Helmuth Lau of 4./KG 2 reported engine problems and failed to return, while Leutnant Wilhelm Pavel's Do 217 from 7./KG 2 is believed to have been hit by anti-aircraft fire and crashed into the sea east of Cromer.

If January 1942 had been quiet, February would be busier, helped in part by Operation *Donnerkeil* – better known as the 'Channel Dash' – on the 12th when the capital ships *Gneisenau*, *Scharnhorst* and *Prinz Eugen* escaped from Brest through the English Channel back to Germany.

The first loss of the month came on 2 February when two Do 217s from 6./KG 40 attacked a convoy off Cromer. No 19 Sqn scrambled two Spitfires from Ludham, in Norfolk, with Plt Offs Maurice Devereux and Jack Henderson then becoming involved in a game of cat and mouse in and out of cloud. Both the Do 217s and the Spitfires quickly separated from each other, and it was Henderson who had the luck when Oberleutnant Ernst Eckert's bomber appeared out of cloud into a patch of blue sky. He immediately turned in behind the aircraft and fired a burst of six seconds, to no apparent effect. Henderson then made a second pass;

'Blue 2 attacked again from the port quarter and fired another long burst with cannon and machine gun from 300-200 yards. As a result, things immediately started to happen. The port engine caught fire, and as Blue 2 continued with his attack, pieces flew off the port engine and a second fire started in either the rear cockpit or the starboard engine. He saw the port engine well alight and small flickering flames coming from the starboard engine. Thin black smoke was issuing from both engines and pieces were still flying off the aircraft. Two of the crew were seen to bail out and the enemy aircraft was last observed gliding down towards the sea in a gentle right hand turn through the cloud.'

Although one of the crew was picked up alive, he later died of exposure.

Three days later it was a repeat performance, this time involving an aircraft from 5./KG 40. Leutnant Gerrit Roosen and his crew, flying in a new Do 217E-4, failed to return from an anti-shipping mission during the afternoon of 5 February. A convoy 20 miles east of Spurn Head, on the Yorkshire coast, reported it was under attack, and two Spitfires from No 133 'Eagle' Sqn flown by Flt Lt Hugh Johnson and Plt Off Marion Jackson and two Hurricanes from No 253 Sqn flown by Plt Off Peter

Oberleutnant Rudolf Häusner (centre, in peaked cap) of 7./KG 2 converses with his groundcrew in front of U5+BR. Another experienced Do 17 and Do 217 pilot, he was killed in action during an attack on York on 17 December 1942

A close-up view of the nose of Do 217E-4 U5+BR of 7./KG 2, photographed at Amsterdam-Schiphol in 1942. It features the KG 2 'Holzhammer' insignia and a yellow diagonal stripe on the nose, with a letter 'B' in white on the lower section of the nose. Note the additional forward armament in the form of an Oerlikon 20 mm MG FF cannon, its barrel protruding through the nose glazing

Landers and Sgt John Tate chased the bomber in and out of cloud. Although none of the RAF pilots actually saw the demise of the Do 217, the destroyer HMS *Mendip* reported seeing a Dornier crash into the sea.

Leutnant Roosen's loss would be the last suffered by II./KG 40 for nearly two months, as the *Gruppe* was detached to Grosseto, in Italy, for much of March so that its crews could be trained on dropping torpedoes – something that had commenced in November 1941 on a *Staffel* by *Staffel* basis. II./KG 40 would never actually undertake such a role in combat, however.

With II./KG 40's frontline strength significantly reduced, KG 2 was tasked with shouldering the burden of operations on the Channel Front. The *Geschwader* duly took its operations further west, with Oberleutnant Rudolf Häusner of 7./KG 2 noting that he moved from Schiphol to Evreux on 7 February to fly just one mission – a diversionary nuisance attack on Exmouth, in Devon, on the 12th (the day of the 'Channel Dash'), before returning to Schiphol 24 hours later. He took off at 0734 hrs and landed at 1010 hrs (German time), and British records acknowledge that Exmouth was attacked just after 0800 hrs when three bombs were dropped, one of which exploded in Bicton Place killing five and injuring seven.

That same day, another nine aircraft attacked Warmwell airfield, in Dorset, and Torquay, in Devon, while a Do 217E-4 of 7./KG 2 flown by Unteroffizier Rolf Güldenpfennig targeted Exeter airfield. Flying at just 100 ft, he approached from the southwest, dropping three bombs on the northern edge of the airfield before being hit by light anti-aircraft fire. The Dornier then collided with a tree and the port wingtip was ripped off, the bomber hitting the ground at a shallow angle and disintegrating over a wide area moments later. Unsurprisingly, the crew were all killed.

On 15 February, an attack on Newcastle would result in the loss of a Do 217 carrying the most senior officer to be killed to date. Major Gerhard Klostermann had taken command of III./KG 2 in September 1941, the 32-year-old being an experienced pre-war fighter and ground attack pilot whose operational flying had only begun in May 1941 when he was posted to KG 2. On the night of the 15th, Klostermann's aircraft (flown by Leutnant Konrad Pellar) and another Do 217 from 9./KG 2, with Unteroffizier Emil Aster at the controls, failed to return and were assumed to have been lost to either ground fire or nightfighters. One claim was submitted by Flg Off James 'Ben' Benson and his radar operator Sgt Lewis Brandon of Beaufighter-equipped No 141 Sqn, who damaged a Do 217 east of Blyth, in Northumberland, at 1950 hrs. This was later upgraded to destroyed, as the local Observer Corps and staff at St Mary's lighthouse, north of Whitley Bay, reported that an aircraft had crashed into the sea four miles east of Blyth at 2006 hrs. No bodies from either crash were ever recovered. Klostermann was replaced by Oberstleutnant Hans von Koppelow, who would then be given command of KG 2 at the start of May 1942.

KG 2 would suffer another four aircraft lost in action off the east coast during the remainder of February. On the afternoon of the 18th, Leutnant Erich Palm of 7./KG 2 failed to return from attacking a convoy in the Humber Estuary. A clue as to what happened to the bomber was given by Unteroffizier Karl Laub of 9./KG 2, who managed to return to Schiphol despite having been attacked by Spitfires. At 1313 hrs, two sections of two fighters from No 609 Sqn took off from Digby, in Lincolnshire, flown by Flg Off 'Joe' Atkinson and Sgt 'Moose' Evans (Red Section) and Flg Offs Yvan du Monceau and 'Balbo' Roeland (Blue Section) and headed for the convoy. The No 609 Sqn Operations Record Book details what then happened;

'The convoy reports a bandit at 3 o'clock and after a while the Duke [du Monceau] sees a Dornier 217 disappear into cloud. He goes above it, sees nothing, then comes down again. Then he sees another Dornier diving, and sighting him, he fires a short burst at 400-300 yards, sees port engine smoke and gives starboard unit a brilliant spray. Soon afterwards convoy reports enemy aircraft shot down by fighters and the Duke finds a patch of oil.'

Meanwhile, Red Section shot up another Do 217, and Wg Cdr Peter Blatchford (the Digby Wing Leader) and Plt Off Christian Ortmans claimed to have damaged a third Dornier.

The next aircraft to be lost was on 24 February, when the Do 217 of Leutnant Ewald Jasper of 7./KG 2 was thought to have been downed by anti-aircraft fire while attacking a convoy off Cromer. However, the bomber was almost certainly shot down by Plt Off Ron Dawson of No 266 Sqn 15 miles northeast of Happisburgh at 1920 hrs. Leutnant Josef Scharnbacher of 9./KG 2 failed to return from mine-laying in the Humber Estuary on the night of 26 February and, finally, Unteroffizier Helmut Günther of 8./KG 2 was also thought to have fallen victim to ground fire 48 hours later on yet another nocturnal mission to the Humber Estuary. Some records suggest that the Do 217 was downed by Sqn Ldr Fred McGevor of Beaufighter-equipped No 255 Sqn, who was himself killed that night after his aircraft was hit by return fire from an unknown opponent and crashed into the sea 36 miles due north of Coltishall, in Norfolk.

February 1942 had seen the most Do 217s available for operations and the most losses to date, but from now on things would change in many ways. Surviving logbooks for March 1942 show little let up in the pace of operations, with Feldwebel Georg Brendebach of 5./KG 2, for example, flying a total of 14 missions during the course of the month – all but two (attacks on Weymouth and Dover) seeing him targeting ships, dropping mines or raiding port towns and cities on the east coast of England. One operation in particular stands out, Brendebach flying to Rennes on 28 March in direct response to the daring commando raid on the dry dock at Saint-Nazaire. Oberleutnant Rudolf Häusner of 7./KG 2 flew just five east coast/mining/anti-shipping missions, while Leutnant Gerhard Blaschke of 5./KG 2 completed a solitary mining mission to the Thames,

KG 2 would carry out regular training missions from Cognac-Châteaubernard airfield in southwestern France. Photographed during just such a flight, this Do 217E-4 (complete with a diagonal band and 'Holzhammer' insignia on its nose) is seen carrying out a mock attack on a U-boat

before heading to Cognac-Châteaubernard to undertake bombing training for the rest of the month.

II./KG 40 also sent aircraft to Rennes following the Saint-Nazaire raid, all II. *Gruppe* Do 217s having by then returned to Soesterberg from Grosseto. Proof of this had come on the night of 26 March when 6./KG 40 lost the E-3 of Leutnant Gerhard Westphal to anti-aircraft fire off Tynemouth, this aircraft being the only Do 217 combat casualty for both units that month. Westphal's body was retrieved from the sea 25 miles northeast of Tynemouth four days later.

With the Do 217 force back to full strength by the beginning of April, operations during the month would push the *Gruppen* equipped with the Dornier bomber to their limit thanks to the initiation of the Baedeker Blitz. On the night of 28–29 March, RAF Bomber Command attacked the city of Lübeck, assessing that 190 acres of the old town were destroyed. German records state that 1425 buildings were destroyed, 1976 seriously damaged and 8411 lightly damaged. Then, on the night of 23–24 April, Rostock was also attacked for the first time. Both cities were former Hanseatic ports, consisting mainly of old, historic buildings. The bombing of Lübeck infuriated Adolf Hitler, who, on 14 April, was responsible for the following signal sent to the Luftwaffe;

'The *Führer* has ordered that the air war against England is to be given a more aggressive stamp. Accordingly, when targets are being selected, preference is to be given to those where attacks are likely to have the greatest possible effect on civilian life. Besides raids on ports and industry, terror attacks of a retaliatory nature are to be carried out against towns other than London.'

The same night that Rostock was initially bombed, the Luftwaffe launched its first retaliatory attack when 48 Do 217s from KG 2 and, possibly, II./KG 40 and 12 Ju 88s from the maritime bomber unit *Kampfgruppe* (KGr) 106 targeted Exeter on 23–24 April. This raid came shortly after Baron Gustav Braun von Sturm, a spokesman for the German Foreign Office, stated, 'We shall go out and bomb every building in Britain marked with three stars in the Baedeker [travel] guide.'

In the three weeks prior to the start of the campaign, KG 2 and II./KG 40 had been highly active attacking maritime targets. By means of example, Feldwebel Georg Brendebach of 5./KG 2 remained in Rennes, from where he attacked Portland naval base, in Dorset, on the night of 2 April, before returning to Soesterberg five days later. He then carried out a further eight missions, either dropping mines or attacking harbours and ports.

KG 2 would lose two aircraft operating against maritime targets before the attack on Exeter. Unteroffizier Fritz Meier of 8./KG 2 was shot down into the Thames Estuary on the night of 5 April by Flg Off Derrick Ryalls in

a Beaufighter of the Fighter Interception Unit (FIU), while Oberleutnant Arnold Goosmann of 7./KG 2 crashed off Cromer two nights later after probably being attacked by Sqn Ldr Richard Trousdale of Beaufighter-equipped No 409 Sqn. However, Trousdale's victim could have also been the Do 217E-4 of *Stab* II./KG 40 flown by *Gruppenkommandeur* Hauptmann Wendt Freiherr von Schlippenbach who failed to return from the same attack on Grimsby, on the Lincolnshire coast. Von Schlippenbach would be replaced by Hauptmann Waldemar Hörner zu Drewer, whose time in command would last just two-and-a-half months.

II./KG 40 also suffered two losses in April, namely Feldwebel Hans Schiff of 4. *Staffel* on the 6th and Leutnant Edgar Scheidhauer from 6. *Staffel* five days later. Both aircraft were conducting operations over the North Sea at the time.

The first Baedeker attack against Exeter was ineffective, with the city avoiding being hit that night – bombs were dropped on Totnes to the southwest, however. Due to overcast skies, ordnance was scattered all over Devon, with just one crew reporting to have bombed the 'city'. Five civilians were killed and eight injured in Totnes. The Luftwaffe lost the aircraft flown by Oberleutnant Dr Kurt Gumbart, who was leading 5./KG 2, to Flg Off John Tharp of No 604 Sqn, whose combat report describing the action reads as follows;

'A silhouette was seen against a dark, starry sky. Beaufighter closed in, saw three exhaust flames, flew underneath enemy aircraft and recognised it as a Do 217. Beaufighter drew back and opened fire from slightly below and dead astern. Flame appeared in the port engine and Beaufighter turned away to right, and then back to watch enemy aircraft, which went vertically down enveloped in flame the whole length of the fuselage. It passed through cloud and then a brilliant flash lit up the sky from below.'

Do 217E-2 Wk-Nr 1145 U5+ZN of 5./KG 2 sits between missions at Soesterberg during the spring of 1942. Lacking camouflage for night operations, the bomber had probably only recently been delivered to 5./KG 2 when this photograph was taken. The aircraft, which was subsequently upgraded into an E-4, was badly damaged after a tyre burst while landing at Vannes on 11 August 1943

The following night (24–25 April), 57 aircraft returned to Exeter, attacking in two waves. This time the raid was more effective, with 6000 houses being damaged, the gas and water pressure reduced due to the mains being hit and four factories receiving modest damage. No fewer than 73 civilians were killed and 54 injured. Not a single claim was made by the RAF and no German aircraft was lost or damaged. It would be a different story in the nights that followed.

On 25–26 April, a major two-wave raid was mounted against Bath, in Somerset. In addition to the usual aircraft from *Luftflotte* 3, a number of bombers from various IV. *Gruppe* (the training *Gruppe* of each *Geschwader*) were involved, flown by both experienced and novice crews. Around 80 aircraft took part, and the historic city suffered significant damage – 250 houses were destroyed and 5000 damaged, and seven factories were hit, with five of them being badly damaged. An electricity power station and a gasworks were also bombed, while communications were badly affected by a direct hit on the city control room. Damage to telephone cables hampered communication with Bristol, the latter city also being attacked but only suffering damage to 700 houses.

The Luftwaffe did not get away scot free, with the only Do 217 lost being the 5./KG 40 machine flown by Feldwebel Herbert Gergs that crashed on its second sortie of the night at Handley Cross, in Dorset. The pilot was apparently dazzled by a searchlight, shortly after which he flew into the ground, killing the entire crew.

The bombers targeted Bath again on the night of 26–27 April, but with less intensity. The attack saw further damage inflicted on residential properties and the main railway station, as well as the Horstman Gear Co Ltd's Newbridge works, which had been damaged in the previous raid. Both nights saw a total of 413 civilians killed and 357 injured. RAF claims during the second Bath attack consisted of an He 111 and a Ju 88 probably destroyed and three Do 217s, a Ju 88 and an He 111 damaged. A single veteran Do 17Z from 10./KG 2 was lost, while an He 111 from IV./KG 4 and another from IV./KG 55 were damaged.

If the RAF was expecting another attack in the West Country on the night of 27–28 April, they were wrong, for during the afternoon of the 27th II./KG 2 moved from Evreux to Soesterberg and III./KG 2 left Caen for Schiphol in preparation for an attack on Norwich, in Norfolk, that evening. A total of 71 aircraft, led by He 111 pathfinders of *Erprobungs-und Lehrkommando* (Erpr.Kdo.)/KG 100, caught the RAF napping during the raid, for no interceptions were made and no German aircraft were lost in combat. Damage was mainly restricted to the poorer residential area of the city, and utility services were only slightly affected. However, the main railway station was burnt out and damage caused to a factory and the BBC buildings in Chapelfield. Some 162 civilians were killed and 600 wounded.

Keeping the British defences guessing as to where would be bombed next, the Luftwaffe targeted York the following night (28–29 April), with 74 aircraft from KG 2, II./KG 40, KGr 106, IV./KG 30, IV./KG 77 and Erpr.Kdo./KG 100 taking part in the raid. The bombers inflicted considerable damage on the historic city, with a large fire being started at the railway station and severe damage caused to the telephone network. A total of 79 civilians were killed and a further 205 wounded.

RAF nightfighters were prepared this time, claiming two Do 217s and two Ju 88s destroyed, two He 111s probably destroyed and two Do 217s damaged. However, the only claim that could be definitely matched to a loss was for the Do 217E-2 flown by Leutnant Karl-Heinz Mühlen of 6./KG 2, the aircraft being shot down by Flg Off Dennis Furse of No 406 Sqn. Mühlen described the final moments of the mission – his 100th operational flight;

'Suddenly, all hell is let loose. Our brave bird trembles under the cannon and machine gun fire of a fighter. The cabin is full of acrid smoke. My composure vanishes immediately. While the bullets strike us, I bank hard right – the fumes disappear. I dive the machine – my Bordmechaniker dangles his left hand in front on me; it is attached to his arm only by shattered skin and bone. I motion to my Beobachter to look out for a second attack but he does not understand and our poor bird receives its death blow. I press back against the armour plating. The machine is shuddering and holes appear in the fuselage, and the canopy beside me looks like a sieve. The port engine has stopped, propeller windmilling in the slipstream.

'Hoping that no vital structural damage has occurred, I bank hard to port and dive steeply to avoid my attacker. Behind me, I see the coast in the moonlight and I start to pull out of my dive at 600 m. I appear to have some elevator control, but as I pull back, the control column comes back into my stomach and we are still diving. I put on full right aileron but the aeroplane still banks to port. "Bail out" I scream. The altimeter reads 150 m – stay in! We are still turning left in a narrow, treeless valley. The cockpit hits the ground, then bounces high, it slides then digs into the earth. The cockpit is partially crushed and I am hanging in my harness. Suddenly, there is a terrific explosion from the main fuel tank. The flash lights up everything like daylight, and then the frightening second is over and finished.'

Three of Mühlen's four-man crew survived the incident, albeit with wounds.

The following night (29–30 April) it was back to Norwich with 70 aircraft. Wg Cdr Peter Prosser Hanks, the Duxford Wing Leader, took off in a Spitfire and claimed two Do 217s probably destroyed and one damaged – just one Dornier from Stab./KG 2 was in fact damaged, the aircraft returning to base with two dead crew. On the ground, Norwich was badly hit, with considerable damage to commercial buildings and residential property. The city's railway goods yard was also damaged and the line connecting Norwich to Cambridge severed, a gas holder in the gasworks destroyed and the waterworks control room demolished, cutting off the water supply to the city centre. As a result of this attack, and the previous raid, 1200 homes had been destroyed and more than 12,500 damaged.

The night of 30 April–1 May saw a temporary shift from Baedeker attacks when 75 aircraft targeted Sunderland and Tyneside. Damage was minimal and the RAF was ready for the raid, with nightfighter crews claiming four He 111s, two Do 217s and a Ju 88 destroyed and five more aircraft damaged. German losses amounted to four Ju 88s, with an He 111 of Erpr.Kdo./KG 100 landing at Ostende with a dead crewman.

The Luftwaffe now took a break of three days before many of its units moved to northern France in order to again attack Exeter. Ninety aircraft took part in the raid on 3–4 May, which would prove to be the most devastating of the three attacks mounted on the city. Fires started in the centre of Exeter developed into a conflagration, and the effective fighting of the blaze was hindered when the Civil Defence Control room had to be evacuated after it caught fire. Railway lines were cratered, gas mains fractured, electricity lines destroyed and severe damage inflicted on seven key sites specifically targeted by the bombers. A total of 400 shops, 150 offices, more than 50 warehouses and 36 pubs and clubs were destroyed, as were 1500 houses, with a further 2700 seriously damaged and 16,000 damaged to a lesser degree.

In human terms, 164 civilians were killed and 563 injured, many of them seriously. Historian Nick Beale recalled what happened to his father Brian, who, then aged 14, was an Air Raid Precaution (ARP) runner that night;

'On the night of the Exeter Blitz, he was woken by the intense light and crackling sound of magnesium parachute flares. He realised what they meant, and reported for duty. All through the bombing, he carried messages between the Heavy Rescue Squad's depot by Polsloe Bridge and the ARP's HQ – a lean-to against the City Library in Castle Street. He was the one who told the HQ personnel the Library itself was on fire — they hadn't realised. The two grown men on duty resorted to strong language, got out in haste and left him there, so he cycled back down Castle Street, with flames from the burning buildings making an arch above his head in the narrow mediaeval street. The road surfaces were so hot that his bike tyres melted – and afterwards the ARP wouldn't pay for new ones.'

Again, the RAF managed to exact some retribution, claiming four Ju 88s and a Do 17 destroyed, with a second Do 17 damaged.

There would be one more attack made during this core period of the Baedeker Blitz when, on the night of 4-5 May, 107 aircraft attacked Cowes, on the Isle of Wight. Two waves of bombers caused widespread damage to property in the town itself, while gas, electricity and water supplies were all affected and eight factories and the gasworks directly hit.

Apparently, the destruction would have been much worse had it not been for the Polish destroyer ORP *Błyskawica*, which was undergoing emergency repairs at the East Cowes shipyard of J Samuel White, where the vessel had been built in 1935–37. Its anti-aircraft guns were in constant action during the attack, so much so that extra ammunition had to be sent across from the mainland. The ship also laid a smoke screen, making it difficult for the German bombers to pinpoint targets in the town. Nevertheless, 65 civilians lost their lives that night, or subsequently died of their injuries. No 604 Sqn's Flt Lt Edward Crew (who had downed a Do 17 during the Exeter raid of the previous night) was credited with the destruction of the Do 217 flown by Feldwebel Ulrich Sonnemann of 9./KG 2, the bomber crashing into the sea off the Isle of Wight.

For the next three months operations would return to normal, even though the Baedeker Blitz actually continued until October 1942, albeit with much less intensity. After a short break, Oberleutnant Rudolf Häusner and his crew from 7./KG 2 recommenced operations in the early hours of

9 May with an attack on Norwich – they noted that the anti-aircraft fire was heavy. Two experienced crews failed to return from the mission. The aircraft of Oberleutnant Werner Böllert of 1./KG 2 collided with a balloon cable and was then hit by fire from a Lewis Gun post, the bomber crashing near Poringland, in Norfolk. The Do 217E-4 of Oberleutnant Hermann Obermeier of 9./KG 2 simply failed to return to base.

The following day, the Häusner crew had their first brush with an RAF fighter. At 1556 hrs, they took off from Schiphol to carry out reconnaissance along the east coast of England. An hour later, a Beaufighter of No 236 Sqn flown by Plt Off Lawrence Lee and Flt Sgt Taylor departed Wattisham, in Suffolk, on a reconnaissance patrol of German convoy routes off the Dutch coast. When the aircraft's radio failed they elected to return to base. At 1712 hrs, flying at just 50 ft above the sea to the east of Great Yarmouth, on the Norfolk coast, Lee and Taylor spotted the Do 217 two miles away flying at the same height.

The Beaufighter gave chase and attacked the bomber from the starboard quarter with a two-second burst that flew over the Dornier. While his crew returned fire, Häusner started taking violent evasive action and soon caught the Beaufighter in his slipstream. Nevertheless, Lee managed to get to within 150 yards of his quarry before opening fire once again, apparently hitting the starboard wing root and causing bits of the aircraft to fly off. Häusner continued to fly erratically, and eventually the Beaufighter's port engine began cutting out, forcing Lee to immediately break off the combat. The undamaged Do 217 landed back at Schiphol 17 minutes after the Beaufighter returned to Wattisham. The Häusner crew had been lucky, and they would continue to be so for the next two months as the sortie rate steadily intensified.

Hull, Poole, Great Yarmouth and Grimsby were attacked during May, and mine-laying missions took place over the Humber (twice) and Thames estuaries. The frequency of operations meant that Do 217s were routinely intercepted by RAF fighters, although II./KG 40 suffered only a single loss during this period. On the evening of 15 May Oberfeldwebel Martin Kalisch of 4./KG 40 was shot down off Happisburgh while searching for a convoy to attack, the bomber being shared between four Spitfires of No 610 Sqn led by Sqn Ldr Gordon Haywood.

The remainder of the month would see KG 2 lose seven Do 217s, including the aircraft of *Staffelkapitäne* Hauptmann Heinrich Schmidt-Hederich of 3./KG 2 (to Spitfires of No 412 Sqn) on the evening of 16 May and Oberleutnant Helmut Voigt of 4./KG 2 on the night of 30 May. In total, the RAF claimed four Do 217s destroyed and one probably destroyed on the 30th, with the Luftwaffe listing the loss of an identical number of Dornier bombers and a lone Ju 88D-1.

In June the Häusner crew attacked Canterbury (twice, as reprisal raids for Bomber Command targeting Cologne), Ipswich, Poole, Southampton and Weston-Super-Mare, and mined the Solent (three times). All the missions were completed without incident apart from the attack on Poole, in Dorset, on the night of 3–4 June. During their return flight to Saint-André-de-l'Eure, in France, the German bombers were followed by two Hurricane intruders of No 1 Sqn flown by Sqn Ldr James MacLachlan and Flt Lt Karel Kuttelwascher. Between them, the RAF fighter pilots claimed to have destroyed three Do 217s and damaged three more in the vicinity of their base. The Häusner crew was forced to divert to Evreux after two Do 217s from KG 2 were shot down (one of which was flown by Feldwebel Franz Koch of 7. *Staffel*, the bomber crashing at Coutances with the death of the whole crew). Three more Dorniers from III./KG 2 and four from II./KG 40 were damaged.

Oberleutnant Karl 'Mano' von Manowarda and his crew also clashed with nightfighters during the summer of 1942, having joined I./KG 2 at the start of May. Von Manowarda had initially been assigned to 5./KG 2 in September 1940, after which he carried out instructor duties prior to conversion onto the Do 217. He had flown an attack on Norwich on 9 May, targeted Southampton on 21 June and then bombed a convoy the following day. The crew's next mission on the night of the 24th would be the first time they attracted the attention of an RAF fighter.

At just before midnight, von Manowarda and his crew took off from Gilze-Rijen, their bomber being one of 80 aircraft from KG 2, I./KG 40, II./KG 77 and KGr 106 bound for Birmingham. 'Mano's' bomb load consisted of a single SC 1200 weapon and two SC 500s. To counter this attack, the RAF launched 54 nightfighters, although only Beaufighter-equipped Nos 25 and 68 Sqns and Mosquitos from No 151 Sqns successfully intercepted the German bombers – five were claimed to have been destroyed, one probably destroyed and one damaged.

The most successful pilot that night was Wg Cdr Irving 'Black' Smith, CO of No 151 Sqn, who remembered the night very well;

'The events are fairly clear to me for two reasons. First, I flew W4095, one of the first nightfighter Mosquitos built. Second, I destroyed the first aircraft with a Mosquito in the war.

A good view of the MG 131 cupola installed in an unidentified Do 217E-4. Numerous access panels on top of the wings and upper fuselage are clearly visible from this angle

'The GCI was Coltishall, and I think the controller was Flt Lt Brown – one of the very few who could think three-dimensionally. He brought me in exactly as I asked him to do in every case. I do not remember the order

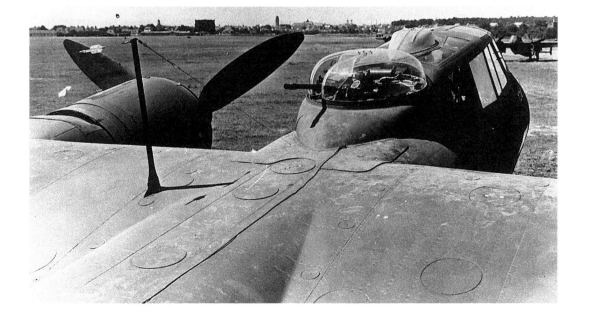

of targets, but the first was a Heinkel [sic]. At night, I always approached at the highest possible speed 1000-2000 ft below what I thought his height to be, as we had no height-finding radar, and pulled up steeply into him at the closest possible range.

'In the first case, I was at approximately the same height, and the target spotted me at about 400 yards, dropped his bombs and went into a very steep diving turn to the left. Because of my high speed, I had a job to follow and shoot before I lost him in a patch of cloud near the sea. The second was copybook. A long burst and the aircraft went straight down and exploded on hitting the sea. The third spotted me, dropped his bombs and bunted. I bunted inside him. I only had two guns working at this time. I could see the strikes on the underside of the wings and he went straight down into the sea, exploded and burned.

'I was covered in lubricating oil from the last target and could no longer see out, so I returned to base.'

Despite the belief there were He 111s flying that night, the reality was that the only aircraft lost were a Do 217 flown by the *Kommandeur* of II./KG 40, Hauptmann Waldemar Hörner zu Drewer, a Ju 88 from 4./KG 77 and two Ju 88s from KGr 106. Another Ju 88 from KGr 106 crash-landed at Schiphol with battle damage from a nightfighter and a Do 217 returned to Gilze-Rijen with dead and wounded crew on board. The latter was the aircraft of von Manowarda, who reported;

Oberleutnant Karl von Manowarda and Feldwebel Ernst Geselle of *Stab* I./KG 2. During the raid on Birmingham on 25–26 June 1942, their Do 217E-4, Wk-Nr 5472 U5+AB, was damaged by a Mosquito from No 151 Sqn. Although von Manowarda managed to nurse the bomber back to Gilze-Rijen, Geselle had been killed by gunfire from the nightfighter

'Over The Wash, we were attacked by a nightfighter. I turned left, dropped the bombs by using the emergency release (reaching for it along with Heinrich Kaiser) and dived. Ernst Fröhlich shouted "He is following us!" I answered "Shoot him down!" and heard Ernst's MG 131 rumble. I flew very low near Norwich and Ipswich – I almost hit a balloon cable south of Ipswich – and then out over the North Sea. I called my crew one after the other, but only the Bordmechaniker did not answer. "Heinrich, go and see what has happened to Ernst Geselle". An anxious silence followed. Heinrich plugged in his intercom "Ernst is dead". I turned towards the British Isles and I thought grimly "You will never see me again – shit England!", but the next evening I was over England again, target Norwich. Filled with bitterness, I hit the centre of this blackened town.

'We buried Ernst in foreign soil on his birthday. Before the flight, he had leaned against me and said he had a premonition of what was going to happen to him over England. We had lain on the ground, he

Hauptmann Alfred Kindler (second from left), *Staffelkapitän* of 6./KG 2, was shot down and taken prisoner on 31 July 1942. He is seen here wearing the *Ritterkreuz* he received while in captivity. To his left is Oberleutnant Hans Wolff of 6./KG 2 who was shot down by a Mosquito of No 157 Sqn on 23 August 1942. They are flanked by two more PoWs from 6./KG 2, namely Leutnante Hartmut Holzapfel (far left, captured on 15 March 1943) and Karl-Heinz Hertam (captured on 15 April 1943)

on my right, using a 500 kg bomb as a pillow. His premonition had been fulfilled.'

Although it is possible that 'Black' Smith attacked von Manowarda's Do 217, it is more likely that the Mosquito that damaged the bomber and killed Ernst Geselle was flown by Sqn Ldr Don Darling. Together with his navigator/radar operator Flg Off Bill Wright, they filed the following combat report;

'A blip was obtained at maximum range below and to starboard at 0118 hrs. Visual followed at 2000 ft, height 5000 ft, of a Do 217. Range was closed to 200 yards and enemy aircraft dived towards cloud. A short burst was fired at it just before it entered cloud until it came out, when another burst was fired as it emerged. Return fire from dorsal turret was experienced but this ceased when strikes were seen on enemy aircraft's fuselage, and it dived to port and disappeared in cloud at 1500 ft and was lost.'

July 1942 would be another bad month for KG 2, which lost 11 aircraft on operations over Britain resulting in the deaths of 39 aircrew, with another five being captured. Amongst the casualties were Hauptmann Walter Frank (*Staffelkapitän* of 1./KG 2) on the night of 21 July, Hauptmann Karl-Heinz Marten (*Staffelkapitän* of 7./KG 2) on the night of 23 July and Hauptmann Alfred Kindler (*Staffelkapitän* of 6./KG 2) on the night of 30–31 July. Kindler and his crew, all whom were captured, were highly experienced, decorated airmen. Indeed, they had all been recipients of the *Deutsches Kreuz* in Gold, and Kindler was subsequently awarded the *Ritterkreuz* in

September of that year. Their aircraft had been hit by anti-aircraft fire as they approached Birmingham, and even though they pressed on to the target, on the way back they knew they could not make it home so bailed out. The abandoned Do 217 crashed near Newmarket.

Aside from the Kindler crew, a further six holders of the *Deutsches Kreuz* in Gold were killed that month – proof that experienced aircrew were also being lost. II./KG 40's casualty rate for July 1942 was slightly better, with just three aircraft being destroyed on operations, seven personnel killed and four captured. It should be stressed that these losses were not because the Do 217 was poorly suited to the tasks being demanded of it. In fact, the Dornier was now the main aircraft striving to carry out the Luftwaffe's mining, anti-shipping and bombing missions against Britain, and crews were having to deal with improved defences assisted by radar. Leutnant Josef Steudel of 8./KG 2 described how his unit attempted to defeat the latter in the summer of 1942;

'Among our experiments was the introduction of *Düppel*. These were black-coloured aluminium strips which had the purpose of jamming the radar. For a while *Düppel* worked well until the "Tommies" managed again to get a step ahead of us and neutralised it. I always felt sorry for the flight engineer – he had to lie on his stomach on the floor with a long carton of *Düppel* beside him. He had to open the door and push the *Düppel* out – a difficult task. At the end of the flight, he would look like a chimney sweep. The whole thing was an emergency improvisation.'

If the surviving Do 217 crews thought that August would bring them better luck, they were in for an unpleasant surprise.

Oberleutnant Rudolf Graf von Thun-Hohenstein had taken command of 7./KG 2 following the death of Hauptmann Karl-Heinz Marten on 24 July. The first three days of August saw von Thun-Hohenstein and his crew target a convoy, bomb Norwich and undertake a daring daylight attack on an airfield near Doncaster. During the latter mission they survived being intercepted by a Spitfire. A second Spitfire, flown by Plt Off Lindsay Black of No 485 Sqn, accounted for the 7./KG 2 Do 217 flown by Unteroffizier Erich Beyerer, the bomber crashing near Kettering. There were no survivors.

The next operation undertaken by KG 2 saw the unit despatch seven Do 217s to attack an armaments factory in Nottingham on 8 August. Taking off from Deelen, in the Netherlands, at 2300 hrs on the 7th, Oberleutnant Rudolf Graf von Thun-Hohenstein's bomber was loaded with four AB 500 incendiary bomb containers. From Deelen, the aircraft flew at low altitude over the North Sea via Texel to the Lincolnshire coast, which they crossed just north of The Wash, and then climbed to 2000 m. It was then that they came under attack.

Earlier that evening, Plt Off Peter Cleaver and Flt Sgt Wallace Nairn of No 68 Sqn had taken off from Coltishall in their Beaufighter on a dusk patrol. At 2315 hrs they were ordered to return to base, although moments later the crew were given a series of vectors that ended with them behind an enemy aircraft at 10,000 ft. Cleaver chased the bomber for 25 minutes, the German pilot jinking his aircraft violently 30-40 degrees to port and starboard and climbing and dropping 1000 ft. The contact was maintained for nine minutes and, at last, Cleaver managed to spot two exhausts per

Flg Off Eric Raybould (left) of No 68 Sqn would be credited with shooting down Oberleutnant Friedrich Dörflinger's Do 217E-4 Wk-Nr 1213 U5+DP of 6./KG 2 on 30 July 1942. The same Beaufighter I, this time flown by Plt Off Peter Cleaver, downed Do 217E-4 Wk-Nr 5455 U5+DR of 7./KG 2 nine days later. Oberleutnant Rudolf Graf von Thun-Hohenstein and his three crew were captured. The two victories are marked on the nose of the nightfighter

engine, only for his quarry to then gradually lose height until it levelled off once again. Closing to 600 ft, Cleaver finally identified the contact as a Do 217 and immediately opened fire from behind with a four-second burst. Strikes were seen all over the aircraft and flames appeared from the port engine and fuselage. The German bomber then dived into cloud.

In the Dornier, bullets went diagonally through the cockpit but no one was hit. The left engine immediately burst into flames and the rudders were no longer functioning. Observer Unteroffizier Horst Arnscheidt pulled the emergency release for the bombs, after which the crew began to bail out. Engineer Feldwebel Helmut Kunze was unable to open the emergency hatch in the floor, so Arnscheidt used his torch to illuminate it so that Kunze could read the instructions. When Kunze finally opened the escape hatch, he immediately fell through the hole together with the door. Radio operator Paulo Bremer had, by then, thrown off the canopy roof, although he chose to jump through the opening in the bottom of the cockpit instead, following Kunze. Arnscheidt released his pilot's seat belts and then bailed out, as did von Thun-Hohenstein.

The No 68 Sqn crew witnessed a large explosion as the Do 217 hit the ground near Revesby, in Lincolnshire. Three or four fires spread over half a mile or more in the vicinity of nearby Coningsby airfield, and the following day, it was confirmed that prisoners had been captured at Revesby Abbey. Amazingly, all four crew survived being shot down.

Operations then tailed off for ten days, with Oberleutnant Mano von Manowarda, now flying with 3./KG 2, only recording a single mission – a search for Feldwebel Georg Zaglmeier and his crew from 2./KG 2 on the 10th. They had been lost the previous night during another attack on Birmingham. Zaglmeier, Oberfeldwebel Helmut Metz of Stab II./KG 40 (targeting Luton) and Feldwebel Philipp Krauschaar of

4./KG 40 (targeting Colchester) had fallen to Beaufighters, with Sqn Ldr Harold Pleasance of No 25 Sqn, Sqn Ldr Bob Braham of No 29 Sqn and Sqn Ldr Bill Beamont of No 219 Sqn each claiming a Do 217 that night. At 0108 hrs on 12 August, an unidentified Beaufighter crew almost certainly claimed the 9./KG 2 aircraft of Leutnant Erich Wolf 100 miles east of The Wash.

The mission tempo increased dramatically once again on 19 August, as Oberleutnant Josef Steudel of 8./KG 2 recalled;

'On the 19th, the British and Canadians attempted a bridgehead at Dieppe. The undertaking, called Operation *Jubilee*, apparently surprised the German high command. KG 2 was sent against the invading troops and suffered severe losses from British fighters. The weakened state which KG 2 then found itself in was evident because very few aircraft were combat ready after Dieppe.'

KG 2 was first informed of the attack at 0722 hrs, and it generated sorties against the invading force until 1900 hrs, when three Do 217s from III./KG 2 targeted retreating ships in Portsmouth harbour. The *Geschwader* lost no fewer than 14 aircraft that day, with a further 13 suffering varying degrees of damage. In human terms, 38 aircrew were killed, five captured and 18 wounded. II./KG 40 fared better, losing three aircraft and having four damaged, with 11 aircrew killed, one captured and two wounded.

Leutnant Josef Steudel joined 8./KG 2 in July 1940, and he would take command of the *Staffel* in July 1943. He later became *Staffelkapitän* of 12./KG 2 in July 1944 and was awarded the *Ritterkreuz* three months later. Steudel survived the war

The RAF claimed to have destroyed 42 Do 217s, probably destroyed a further six and damaged 48. Clearly, there was much over-claiming, so identifying exactly who downed whom is virtually impossible, apart from the loss of the aircraft flown by Oberleutnant Adolf Wolff of 5./KG 40. Having rushed to get airborne from Soesterberg to search for Allied warships that might be headed for Dieppe from ports on the east coast of England, Wolff and his crew were returning to base when they spotted two twin-engined fighters, which immediately attacked. Flg Off John Bryan and Sgt Desmond Roberts of Whirlwind-equipped No 137 Sqn noted what happened next in their joint combat report;

'Section dived and identified enemy aircraft as a Do 217, which turned across to starboard, firing from top turret and climbing. Red 2 gave a four-second burst from 200 yards, observing no results. Red 1 made a steep turn to starboard, coming in to dead astern slightly below, Do 217 jinking and firing continuously from bottom turret. Red 1 gave a three-second burst from 250 closing to 200 yards, observing strikes on underside of rear half of the fuselage and port engine and pieces falling off enemy aircraft.

He gave a further two bursts, finishing his ammunition from dead astern, seeing strikes underneath fuselage near cockpit and pieces falling off. Red 1 then broke away and Red 2 came in line astern, and diving slightly, gave three bursts from 300 closing to 200 yards, observing strikes underneath and on top, smoke and pieces falling off.

'Four crew now bailed out from 1500 ft, parachutes being seen to open. The first to bail out had a large hole in the parachute. Red 2 broke away to starboard and came in again from port, enemy aircraft now in flames, pulled up sharply, stalled and dived straight into the sea.'

Wolff, unwounded, was the only survivor. He spent the rest of the war as a PoW.

An unnamed Do 217 crewman from KG 2 who was subsequently captured later that year gave his interrogators details about how the losses on 19 August had affected his *Geschwader*;

'The strength of both II. and III./KG 2 has become quite seriously depleted. Prior to Dieppe, 6./KG 2, which was the strongest in II./KG 2, had not more than seven or nine aircraft and crews. Three of these failed to return from operations at Dieppe, and a fourth crashed near Amiens and exploded just after the crew, one of whom was seriously wounded, got clear. III./KG 2 was in a worse condition. At the time of Dieppe, one *Staffel* was down to three crews, two of whom were on leave and, according to a prisoner, the total strength of the *Gruppe* was scarcely more than the equivalent of one full *Staffel*.'

Hauptmann Walter Bradel was initially a transport pilot before transferring to command 9./KG 2 in September 1940. Awarded the *Ritterkreuz* on 17 September 1941, he became *Gruppenkommandeur* of II./KG 2 in December 1941 and *Geschwaderkommodore* of KG 2 in January 1943. Bradel was killed in an accident returning from operations on 4 May 1943

The next loss suffered by KG 2 involved yet another experienced crew. Oberleutnant Hans Walter Wolff had been awarded the *Frontflugspange* in Gold for completing 110 operational flights by mid-September 1941, which followed his receipt of the *Ehrenpokal* three months earlier – Wolff would be awarded the *Deutsches Kreuz* in Gold in December 1942. Due to his crew's experience, Wolff and his men were posted to 10./KG 2 at Achmer-Bramsche in December 1941 to serve as instructors. Returning to 6./KG 2 in August 1942, he would then take temporary command of 6./KG 2 after Hauptmann Alfred Kindler became a PoW on 31 July.

An attack on the Unicam works northeast of Cambridge on the night of 22 August would be Wolff's 154th and, as it would transpire, last mission of the war. At about 2000 hrs, four crews from II./KG 2 were hurriedly briefed for the attack by Wolff, who had only recently been told the mission specifics by the *Gruppenkommandeur*, Hauptmann Walter Bradel. Each observer was issued with large-scale maps and told to be sure of their target – the Unicam factory near the Chesterton Fen Road viaduct over the River Cam.

Carrying four 500 kg bombs, Wolff made landfall at Orford Ness, in Suffolk, at 10,000 ft and, with good visibility, began to descend towards Cambridge. Just as they had reached 5000 ft, they were caught unawares by a Mosquito of No 157 Sqn flown by Wg Cdr Richard Slade and radar operator Plt Off Philip Truscott. The pair had taken off on patrol at 2053 hrs, and when 25 miles east of Southwold were vectored onto Wolff's Do 217, which was about 12 miles from the coast. They then stalked the German bomber, and when sure it was hostile, Slade engaged the Do 217 at 2240 hrs;

'I fired from 500 ft with cannon only for two to three seconds, holding him in my sights the whole time. Strikes were seen on the port side of the fuselage and centre section, and as he fell away after I ceased fire, an enormous shower of sparks shot out, apparently from his port side. He dived away to starboard so fast it was impossible to get a deflection shot in. His silhouette was lost against the dark ground, but some very dim lights appeared on his wing tips, suggesting formation lights having been knocked on. There was also a faint glow from the fuselage or an engine, which I would not have claimed as a fire. Further isolated sparks flew out at some distance as the enemy aircraft went down.'

The attack came as a complete surprise to the Dornier crew. Wolff managed to dive steeply, but with a burning engine. He tried to regain control, although knew it was pointless, so he jettisoned the bombs and, when at 2000 ft, ordered the crew to bail – one had to be literally kicked out as he was scared to jump. On landing, all four airmen met up and decided to hand themselves in to the nearest police station, where they were courteously received and offered a biscuit and a cup of tea.

KG 2 would lose two more aircraft the following night, whose observers were *Deutsches Kreuz* in Gold recipient Oberleutnant Richard Scheurer of 1. *Staffel* and *Staffelkapitän* of 2./KG 2, Hauptmann Rudolf Hellmann. Oberleutnant von Manowarda took part in a fruitless air-sea rescue search for both crews the following day. RAF nightfighters claimed to have destroyed two Do 217s, probably destroyed a third and damaged two. KG 2 had two more bombers downed on operations on the night of 28 August.

A similar pattern of attacks and attrition would follow in September, with KG 2 losing four Do 217s and II./KG 40 one. One of the aircraft downed was the E-4 of Feldwebel Alfred Witting on the night of the 8th, which fell to Flg Off Alexander McRitchie of No 151 Sqn. Confusingly, the bomber was recorded as belonging to both 3./KG 2 and 6./KG 40. It appears that Witting was at the controls of an aircraft carrying II./KG 40's 'F8' code, which means that there was either a shortage of aircraft in KG 2 at the time, or he was flying with the latter unit in order to gain combat experience. Witting and his crew were killed when the Dornier crashed near Orwell, in Cambridgeshire.

KG 2's final loss of the month involved the aircraft flown by Feldwebel Ferdinand Handel of 1. *Staffel*, the bomber mounting a rare daylight attack on a factory in Penzance, in Cornwall, on 26 September with 24 other Do 217s from I. and III./KG 2. The aircraft was attacked by a Beaufighter of No 406 Sqn and crashed in St Just, killing three of the four crew. I. and III./KG 2 had moved to Evreux two days before the raid, and they would return to Holland during the afternoon of the 27th.

The mission tempo tailed off in October, (*text continues on page 43*)

COLOUR PLATES

1
Do 217 V4 Wk-Nr 690 D-AMSD of the *Erprobungsstelle der Luftwaffe*, Rechlin, Germany, June 1939

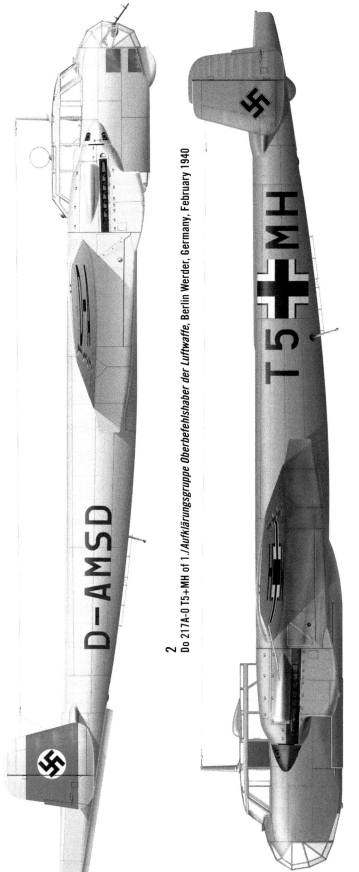

2
Do 217A-0 T5+MH of 1./*Aufklärungsgruppe Oberbefehlshaber der Luftwaffe*, Berlin Werder, Germany, February 1940

3
Do 217E-1 Wk-Nr 5069 U5+DN of 5./KG 2, Evreux, France, October 1941

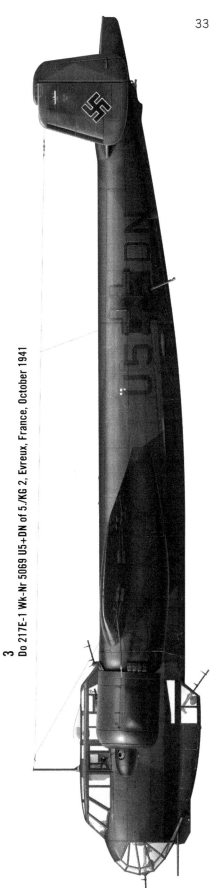

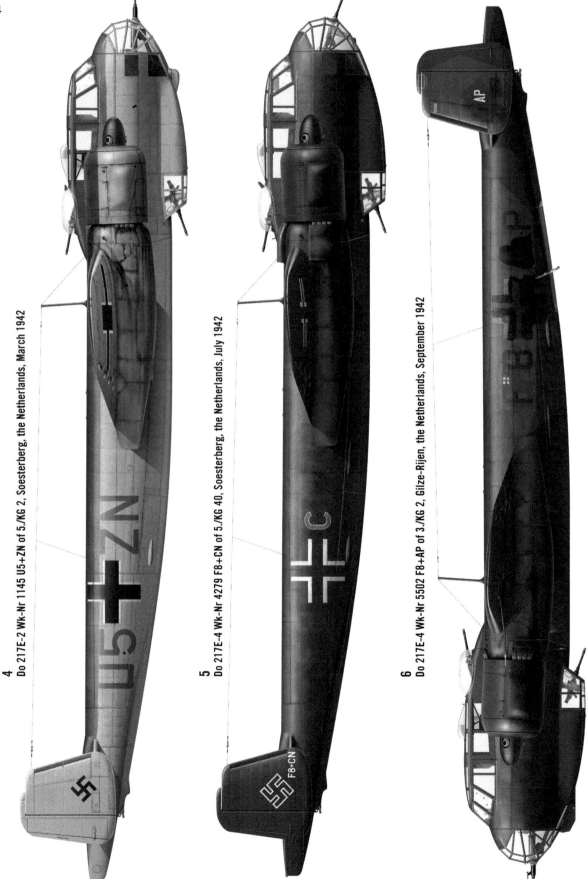

4
Do 217E-2 Wk-Nr 1145 U5+ZN of 5./KG 2, Soesterberg, the Netherlands, March 1942

5
Do 217E-4 Wk-Nr 4279 F8+CN of 5./KG 40, Soesterberg, the Netherlands, July 1942

6
Do 217E-4 Wk-Nr 5502 F8+AP of 3./KG 2, Gilze-Rijen, the Netherlands, September 1942

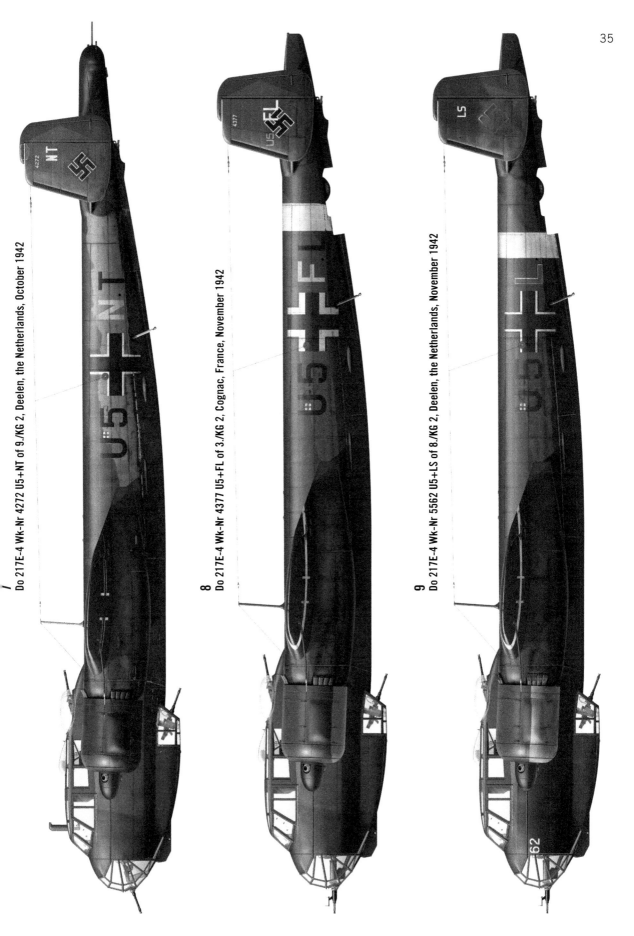

7
Do 217E-4 Wk-Nr 4272 U5+NT of 9./KG 2, Deelen, the Netherlands, October 1942

8
Do 217E-4 Wk-Nr 4377 U5+FL of 3./KG 2, Cognac, France, November 1942

9
Do 217E-4 Wk-Nr 5562 U5+LS of 8./KG 2, Deelen, the Netherlands, November 1942

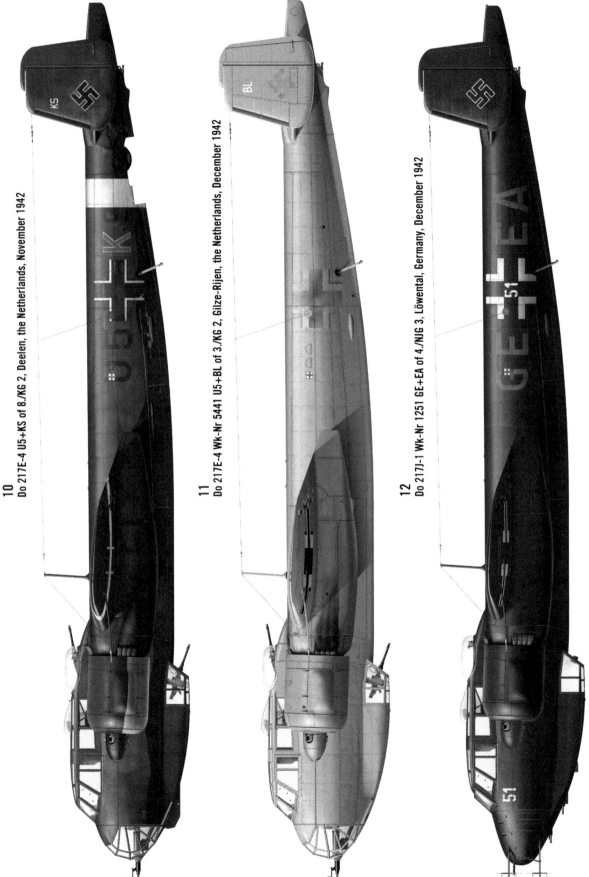

10
Do 217E-4 U5+KS of 8./KG 2, Deelen, the Netherlands, November 1942

11
Do 217E-4 Wk-Nr 5441 U5+BL of 3./KG 2, Gilze-Rijen, the Netherlands, December 1942

12
Do 217J-1 Wk-Nr 1251 GE+EA of 4./NJG 3, Löwental, Germany, December 1942

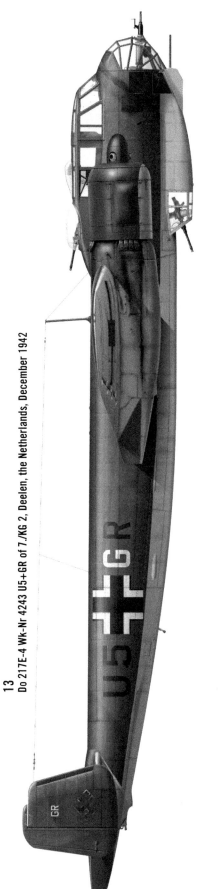

13
Do 217E-4 Wk-Nr 4243 U5+GR of 7./KG 2, Deelen, the Netherlands, December 1942

14
Do 217K-06 Wk-Nr 4406 RD+IE of *Kampfgruppe zur besonderen Verwendung* 21, Schwäbisch Hall, Germany, January 1943

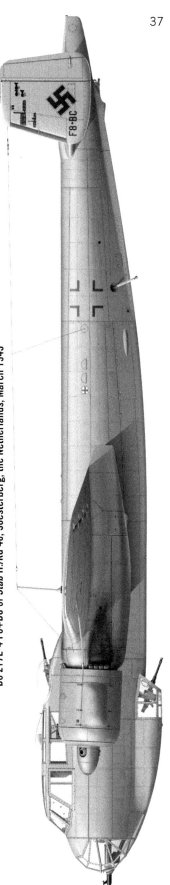

15
Do 217E-4 F8+BC of *Stab* II./KG 40, Soesterberg, the Netherlands, March 1943

38

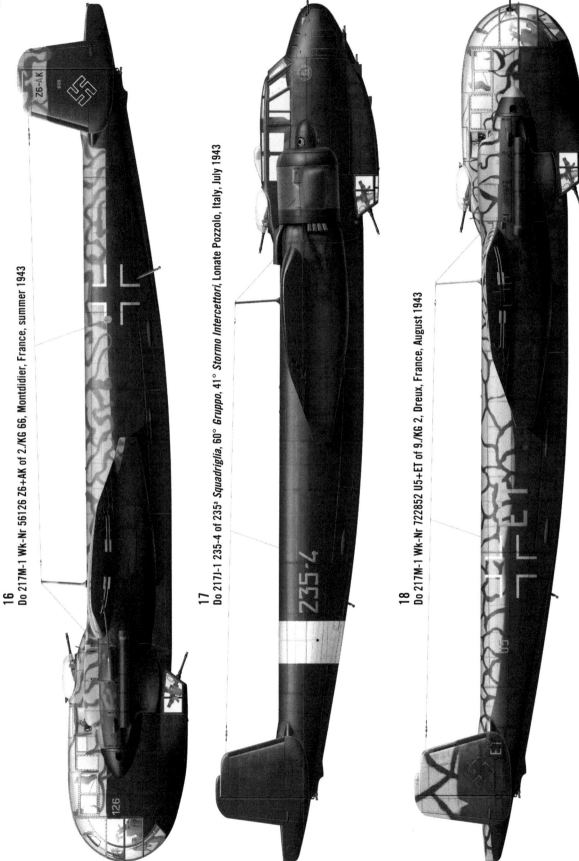

16
Do 217M-1 Wk-Nr 56126 Z6+AK of 2./KG 66, Montdidier, France, summer 1943

17
Do 217J-1 235-4 of 235ª *Squadriglia*, 60° *Gruppo*, 41° *Stormo Intercettori*, Lonate Pozzolo, Italy, July 1943

18
Do 217M-1 Wk-Nr 722852 U5+ET of 9./KG 2, Dreux, France, August 1943

19
Do 217M-1 Wk-Nr 56125 U5+UK of 2./KG 2, Eindhoven, the Netherlands, September 1943

20
Do 217E-5 Wk-Nr 5654 6N+NP of 6./KG 100, Istres, France, September 1943

21
Do 217E-4 Z6+DH of 1./KG 66, Montdidier, France, September 1943

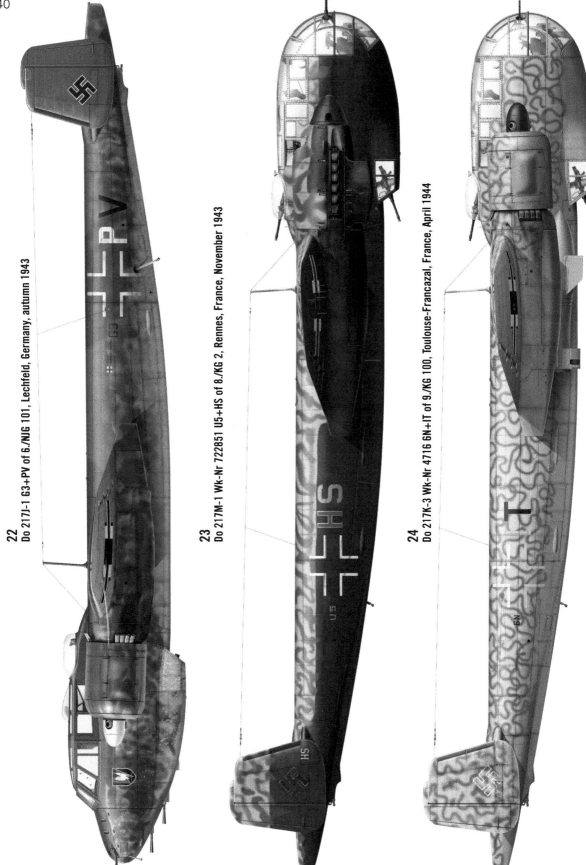

22
Do 217J-1 G3+PV of 6./NJG 101, Lechfeld, Germany, autumn 1943

23
Do 217M-1 Wk-Nr 722851 U5+HS of 8./KG 2, Rennes, France, November 1943

24
Do 217K-3 Wk-Nr 4716 6N+IT of 9./KG 100, Toulouse-Francazal, France, April 1944

25
Do 217K-3 Wk-Nr 4749 6N+HR of 9./KG 100, Toulouse-Francazal, France, May 1944

26
Do 217N-1 Wk-Nr 1570 3C+IP of 6./NJG 6, Tavaux, France, May 1944

27
Do 217M-1 Wk-Nr 56347 K7+LH of 1./*Nachtaufklärungsstaffel*, Copenhagen, Denmark, May 1945

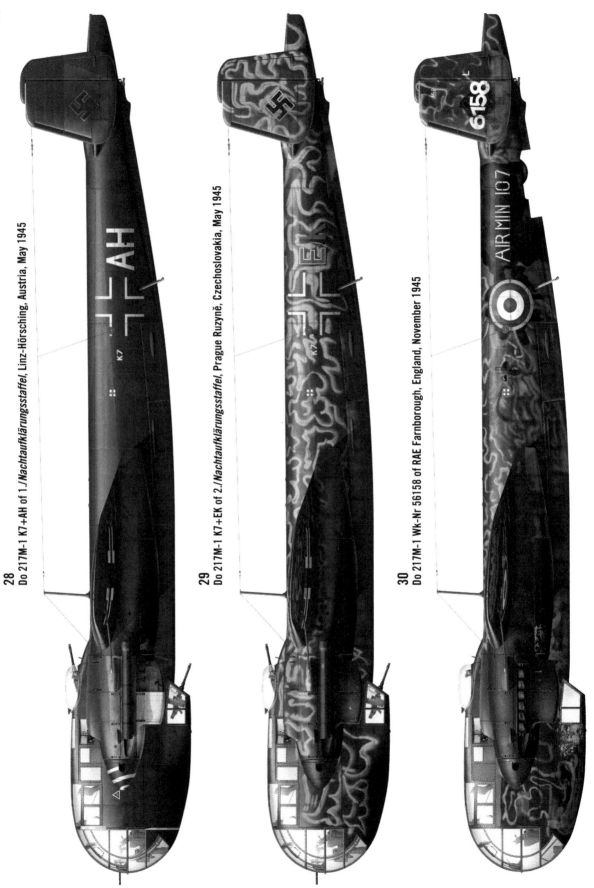

28
Do 217M-1 K7+AH of 1./*Nachtaufklärungsstaffel*, Linz-Hörsching, Austria, May 1945

29
Do 217M-1 K7+EK of 2./*Nachtaufklärungsstaffel*, Prague Ruzyně, Czechoslovakia, May 1945

30
Do 217M-1 Wk-Nr 56158 of RAE Farnborough, England, November 1945

The remains of Do 217E-4 Wk-Nr 4289 U5+IS of 8./KG 2 at Rochford airfield shortly after it was brought down by anti-aircraft fire on the afternoon of 26 October 1942. The bomber was hit as it flew at low-level over the RAF fighter base, sliding at high-speed across the ground until it crashed into a brick-built dispersal hut. Unteroffizier Rudolf Schumann and his crew were either killed outright in the crash or later succumbed to injuries

resulting in the first loss for either *Geschwader* not occurring until the 26th. Unteroffizier Rudolf Schumann of 8./KG 2 had been briefed to carry out a daylight attack on the Skefko Ball Bearing Company factory in Luton. A total of six bombers were scheduled to take part in the operation, but only two departed Deelen at 1130 hrs due to bad weather. As Schumann approached the coast, conditions deteriorated further to the point where the crew abandoned the planned attack and crossed the coast at Southend, in Essex, at 200 ft. They dropped their bombs near Rochford Hospital and then, turning steeply, flew at very low-level over nearby Rochford airfield. The aircraft was hit by fire from quadruple Vickers machine guns and Bofors guns, killing Schumann and causing the bomber to immediately crash-land. The Do 217 skidded along the ground until it hit a brick dispersal hut, killing two more of the crew. The radio operator, Gefreiter Heinz Kautz, was thrown clear of the wreckage, although he succumbed to his injuries on 25 January 1943.

Five more Do 217s were lost on 31 October–1 November when two waves of aircraft attacked Canterbury at night after 30 Fw 190 *Jabos* had targeted the city that afternoon. Both of the downed bombers, from 7./KG 2 (although one wore the 'F8' code of II./KG 40), were part of the first wave, and they crashed into the sea east off Foreness, in Kent. Three Dorniers from I./KG 2 were lost in the second wave, with the aircraft of Oberfeldwebel Peter Metzenroth crashing near Bridge, in Kent. Three of the Do 217s were claimed by No 29 Sqn pilots Sqn Ldr Bob Braham and Flg Off George Pepper, the latter being credited with single bombers from both waves.

Although November had started badly for KG 2, it would lose only one more Do 217 during the rest of the month. Gefreiter Heinrich Kuhlmann's 8. *Staffel* aircraft was hit in the cockpit by the first shell fired from a Bofors gun as the bomber crossed the coast west of Folkestone, in Kent, at just 70 ft at 1450 hrs on 5 November. The Do 217 crashed shortly thereafter, killing the crew.

Three days later, the Allies landed in Morocco and Algeria at the start of Operation *Torch*. The Germans launched Operation *Stockdorf* in response, and this saw all three *Gruppe* of KG 2 and II./KG 40 hastily transferred to Cognac-Châteaubernard when it was feared that the Allies could also invade southern France. However, after flying just two uneventful missions from here, all the Do 217s had returned to Holland by 3 December.

The final month of 1942 would see a resumption of the attacks on east coast targets and the recommencement of aerial mining of The Wash and the Thames Estuary. There was also an increase in what were known as 'Pirate' attacks – isolated daylight raids on specific targets by experienced crews. An airman captured in August 1942 described the specifics of such attacks;

'Suitable targets are selected many weeks in advance and intensive preparations are made. Very careful thought is given to the choice of route and large-scale maps and any available photographs of the target itself, and the approaches to it, are closely studied. III./KG 2 even had a special sand-table prepared for use in connection with "Pirate" attacks. Pains are taken to work out a route which runs over flat country and which avoids any hills or other natural or artificial obstructions. Towns are studiously avoided. A hand drawn sketch is frequently made covering a strip eight miles wide

Photographed in November 1942, these Do 217E-4s are from 8./KG 2. The furthest aircraft, U5+KS, still has the Operation *Stockdorf* white band around the wings and tail and yellow undersides to the engine cowlings. The nearest bomber is 'flying' an 8. *Staffel* pennant above the cockpit. The pennant features a shield with a sword piercing a red number '8' and a yellow map of Britain on a white background, behind which are yellow/red/yellow horizontal stripes

on either side of the route, and all of the crew are expected to memorise the landmarks along the entire route. As many as three aircraft may be despatched to attack an important objective, but it is considered preferable to decide upon several different targets to be attacked by individual aircraft on the same day.'

At the start of December, Oberleutnant Mano von Manowarda had just returned I./KG 2 after spending several months with 15./KG 6 at Chartres training crews to fly the Do 217. He participated in an attack on Sunderland and Hartlepool on 12 and 14 December, and on the 16th flew his first 'Pirate' attack. He provided details of the missions in a letter he wrote to the author in the 1980s;

'I am still today worried about a low-level attack (by the order of the *Führer*) on the small town of Wareham. There, I dropped four 500 kg bombs precisely. Even now I can see the people going to the market without any air raid warning being heard, and in particular a mother with a small child at her right hand. I dropped the bombs (fuses without delay), banked to port and flew high up so that the explosions did not hit us. I cannot forget this terror attack.'

A report filed by the Dorset Constabulary the following day acknowledges the attack, but the outcome was slightly different to what Mano thought;

'At 1333 hrs on 16 December 1942, a Do 217 machine-gunned the town of Wareham and dropped four 500 kg armour piercing bombs. Five dwelling houses were demolished and approximately 80 damaged.

Photographed at Gilze-Rijen in December 1942, this Do 217E-4 of 3./KG 2 is camouflaged in the overall pale grey scheme adopted for daylight 'Pirate' attacks by solitary Dorniers against specific targets. Relying on bad weather for cover, only experienced crews usually undertook such missions. The pilot of this aircraft was Oberleutnant Ernst Schneiderbauer (second from left, facing the camera), who had flown Fw 200s with I./KG 40 prior to being transferred to I./KG 2. He was shot down and taken prisoner on the night of 11 March 1943

A gasometer was burnt out and damage was caused to overhead telephone wires. Casualties – two persons seriously injured, 12 slightly injured.'

The following day, the Chief Constable of Dorset sent his daily report to the Home Office. It listed three attacks by German bombers on 16 December. In addition to Mano's attack, there was an almost simultaneous raid on Bridport that caused extensive damage and chaos, with three civilians killed, seven seriously injured and ten slightly injured. However, it was the attack on Poole that was most effective, as his report explains;

'At 1323 hrs, a Do 217 flying from northeast to southwest at 1500 ft machine-gunned and dropped four 500 kg bombs on the harbour area at Poole. A number of workshops and stores were demolished or partly demolished, and warehouses, workshops, stores, dwelling houses, shops and other buildings were damaged. One naval vessel was sunk and others damaged. Two persons killed, three seriously injured and 23 slightly injured. The Dorset Foundry factory, which is engaged on work of national importance, was one of those damaged.'

Bombs landed close to the Poole gasworks, hit the Dorset Foundry in Thames Street and badly damaged the quayside site of Newman's Shipyard – the vessel *Vixen Hamworthy* was also sunk here. However, nothing further was known at that time as to the identity of the crew that attacked Poole until the discovery of an account written by German war reporter Günther Niemeyer. This, and a paragraph in the intelligence debrief of an Austrian bomber pilot captured on 11 March 1943, positively identified the attacker as Oberleutnant Ernst Schneiderbauer in a Do 217E-4 of 3./KG 2.

Schneiderbauer had joined the *Staffel* in the summer of 1942, having previously flown Fw 200s on armed reconnaissance missions over the Atlantic. By the time he was shot down on 11 March 1943, he had completed more than 100 operational flights and listed Lincoln, Canterbury, Grimsby, Plymouth, Portsmouth, Southampton, London and Swansea as his night targets. Schneiderbauer had also flown a number of attacks by daylight, bombing Norwich, Chatham, Southampton, Bexhill, Chelmsford and, of course, Poole on 16 December. The British intelligence report on the latter raid noted;

'The Poole incident was directed against a small ship-building yard. Four 500 kg bombs were dropped which the pilot thought straddled the target. This incident is confirmed by British sources, from which it is learned that at 1337 hrs on the day in question, three bombs were dropped on the quayside at Poole and one in the main harbour.'

Not all the 'Pirate' attacks met with success on the 16th, however. At 1355 hrs, the No 141 Sqn crew of Flg Off Bill Cook and Flt Sgt Len Warner had been scrambled from Ford, in West Sussex, in their Beaufighter. Having failed to intercept any enemy aircraft due to poor weather conditions, they were heading back to base when, at 1448 hrs, they spotted a lone Do 217 flying west at low-level. They immediately gave chase, following the wildly weaving aircraft that was machine-gunning houses from an altitude of 30-50 ft. The Beaufighter followed at 150 ft, Cook waiting for the Do 217 to climb.

As they headed for Bognor Regis, the Do 217 turned sharply to starboard, then to port, which put the bomber in line with the Bognor Regis gasworks. The pilot, Unteroffizier Ernst Dittrich of 4./KG 40,

The port vertical tail fin of Do 217E-4 F8+BC of *Stab* II./KG 40 was adorned with the victory tally of veteran pilot Hauptmann Wilhelm Schmitter. The aircraft was camouflaged in 'Pirate' pale grey overall, which meant the victory markings stood out even more than usual. Schmitter's tally in early 1943 comprised two victory bars (from 15 August 1940 and 1 July 1941), two factory attacks (believed to be Leamington Spa on 13 June and 16 July 1942) and three barrage balloons destroyed – not all in this Do 217, however

who, along with his crew, was on his first operational flight, saw that the bomber's starboard wing would hit the gasometer, so he tried to correct his turn by throttling back and swinging the aircraft to starboard. However, the wingtip clipped the gasometer, spinning the Dornier around and crashing the cockpit section of the aircraft into a smaller gasometer – there were no survivors. The chase had lasted a mere two minutes.

Dittrich's Dornier was the fourth Do 217 lost in December, and a further five would be destroyed before month's end. Two of these aircraft were lost on the night of the 17th during an attack on York. Although Mano von Manowarda recorded that he had successfully dropped a 1200 kg and two 500 kg bombs on the target, the aircraft flown by Feldwebel Wilhelm Stoll of 2./KG 2 and the experienced Hauptmann Rudolf Häusner, *Staffelkapitän* of 7./KG 2, inexplicably flew into hillsides on the North Yorkshire moors, killing all eight crew. The evidence of Häusner's crash is still visible at Hawnby, with a gap in the dry stone wall he hit exactly matching the wingspan of a Do 217.

The following day, Unteroffizier Walter Seideler of II./KG 40 was shot down south of the Isle of Wight by a Typhoon flown by Plt Off Gordon Thomas of No 486 Sqn. Then, on 22 December, Leutnant Eberhard Bergmann of 2./KG 2 and Leutnant Heinz-Wolf Krabbenhöf of 4./KG 40 failed to return from 'Pirate' attacks on targets on the West Sussex coast, both aircraft being downed by Typhoons 15 miles south of Selsey. Their demise was credited to No 486 Sqn pilots Flg Off 'Spike' Umbers and Flt Sgt Charles Gall.

Although these aircraft would be the last Do 217s lost in combat in 1942, the final Dornier to be destroyed that year was the machine of Leutnant Hermann Brockhage and his crew from 1./KG 2 on 30 December. Upon returning to Gilze-Rijen after a low-level training flight over the Zuiderzee, Brockhage clipped the house at 94 Keizer Ottostraat, in Bussum, and crashed, killing him and his crew.

1942 had been a hard year for KG 2 and II./KG 40, and 1943 would bring more of the same, as well as changes. Indeed, II./KG 40's association with the Do 217 would last only until the start of June. A small number of new units would also be equipped with the Dornier, and they would use the aircraft to carry out a variety of roles with varying degrees of success.

CHAPTER THREE

NEW DEVELOPMENTS

A number of developments for the tried and tested Do 217E-4, most of which came to fruition from late 1942, would now influence the design and future use of the aircraft.

In response to the intensifying night offensive by Bomber Command against targets in Germany, additional nightfighters were urgently required by the Luftwaffe. In the summer of 1940, the need for such aircraft had resulted in the development of two versions of the Do 17 to undertake this role to complement the Bf 110 and Ju 88C. These were the Do 17Z-7 Kauz (Screech Owl) I and the Z-10 Kauz II, which had the glazed nose of the standard Do 17Z-3 replaced by the solid, armament-equipped (three 7.92 mm machine guns and one 20 mm cannon) nose from the Ju 88C-2/4. The Z-7 was soon found to be underarmed, so an entirely new nose design was created that increased the armament to four machine guns and two cannon. An infra-red Spanner Anlage illuminator was installed in the tip of the nose, although this was later replaced by first-generation FuG 202 Lichtenstein radar equipment. The new Dornier nightfighter was designated the Do 17Z-10.

With the Do 17Z being replaced in the frontline by the Do 217E, production of the original Dornier bomber ended in October 1940. A Do 217E-1 was subsequently used to assess the suitability of the type as a nightfighter. In February 1942, a Do 217E-2 was fitted with FuG 202 Lichtenstein BC radar and Spanner Anlage, the aircraft later

Do 217J-1 Wk-Nr 1251 GE+EA of 4./NJG 3 was fitted with FuG 202 Lichtenstein radar. Almost certainly featuring codes and spinners in red, the nightfighter was badly damaged at Westerland-Sylt on 9 July 1942. It subsequently suffered a second accident with I./NJG 4 on 22 January 1943 and was finally written off on 26 March 1944 while serving with II./NJG 101

Hauptmann Wilhelm Herget (far right) was an experienced day and nightfighter pilot who would end the war with 15 day and 58 night victories, for which he was awarded the *Ritterkreuz mit Eichenlaub*. He was not an advocate of the Do 217 as a nightfighter, preferring the Bf 110

being re-designated the Do 217J-1. Its armament consisted of four 7.92 mm MG 17 machine guns and four MG FF 20 mm cannon in a solid nose, with the latter weapons eventually being replaced by four MG 151s. The E-2's rear-firing guns, including the turret-mounted MG 131, were retained, as was the ability to carry bombs, for the aircraft was initially intended to operate as a night intruder. However, prior to its first flight, in October 1941, such missions over Britain had ceased by order of the *Führer*. So, unlike the Do 17Z-10 and Ju 88C-2/6, the J-1 was never used in the intruding role. The Do 217J-2 that soon followed differed from J-1 in that it was fitted with FuG 212 Lichtenstein C-1 radar.

Operational evaluation of the aircraft was carried out in March 1942 when Do 217J-1s were issued to Oberleutnant Wilhelm Herget's 4. *Nachtgeschwader* (NJG) 1. Herget, himself, was not a fan of the Dornier, and later wrote;

'My *Gruppe* had a *Staffel* of Do 217s because Bf 110s were in short supply, and High Command thought that the aircraft's four-and-half-hour endurance compared to the two-and-a-half hours of the Bf 110 could be of use. The 217 was fast, stable, excellent for instrument flying and obviously a very nice bomber, but much too heavy on the controls for a fighter. I flew it once just to try it, but after that I refused to use it on operations and stuck to my tried and tested 110, which was greatly superior as a fighter.'

Pilots generally found the aircraft to be a handful when taking off and landing, and once in the air, it had too little performance in reserve to function effectively as a fighter. Furthermore, being fitted with both offensive and defensive armament, the Do 217J routinely

carried 750 kg of ammunition. This in turn meant that the nightfighter lacked the manoeuvrability required to be successful in combat against enemy bombers.

On 31 July 1942, the Do 217N-1 flew for the first time, this aircraft being identical to the J-2 but with more powerful 1849 hp DB 603A-1 inline engines installed in place of the 1539 hp BMW 801L radials. The follow-on N-2 would later have the turret and rear-facing guns removed, and many were fitted with obliquely- mounted upward-firing MG 151 cannon in the fuselage as part of the so-called *Schräge Musik* modification. This unique armament fit had been championed by Oberleutnant Rudolf Schoenert of 4./NJG 2 in July 1942 – the same month he was awarded the *Ritterkreuz* for having shot down 21 aircraft by night.

Schoenert, who later flew with 2./NJG 3, II./NJG 5 and I./NJG 100, was, surprisingly it would appear, a great supporter of the Do 217 nightfighter, and it is thought that 27 of his 65 victories came when he was flying the aircraft. Of those, 25 were claimed over the Eastern Front when he commanded I./NJG 100 from August 1943 through to January 1944, Schoenert shooting down a total of 31 aircraft between 16 August and 27 October 1943.

Leutnant Johann Krause was another nightfighter pilot to enjoy success with the Do 217. Having joined I./NJG 3 in November 1941, he would commence his conversion onto the Dornier from the Bf 110 with 7./NJG 1 on 19 June 1942. Returning to I./NJG 3 to fly his first operational mission with the aircraft on 27 August, Krause's first victory with the Do 217 came on 6 October when he shot down two Wellingtons. Posted to Dornier-equipped 6./NJG 101 in May 1943, he failed to add to his tally until 1 February 1944. Five months later Krause began flying the Ju 88, although by then he had shot down 14 aircraft with the Do 217.

Combat accounts from RAF crews engaged by Do 217s are rare. One of the few such encounters to be recorded came during a mission to Schweinfurt on 24 February 1944. A No 619 Sqn Lancaster flown

Do 217N-2 Wk-Nr 0174 PE+AW was a conversion of a Do 217E-1. Note that the aircraft is not fitted with radar

OPPOSITE
Do 217J-1 235-4 of 235ª *Squadriglia*, 60° *Gruppo*, 41° *Stormo Intercettori* belly-landed near its airfield at Lonate Pozzolo in late July or early August 1943 while being flown by unit CO Capt Aramis Ammanato, who later reported that he could not lower the undercarriage due to the presence of metallic fragments in the landing gear's hydraulic system. It was one of 12 Do 217 nightfighters (six J-1s and six J-2s) delivered to 235ª *Squadriglia*

by Flg Off Keith Williams had taken off from Coningsby, in Lincolnshire, at 2008 hrs, and the flight was uneventful for the first few hours until the bomber approached the town of Calw, west of Stuttgart, when all hell broke loose.

Oberleutnant Wilhelm Welk of 5./NJG 101 had taken off in his Do 217 from München-Riem and was soon vectored onto a target. At 2250 hrs, he opened fire on a bomber and saw hits on the port wing. In the Lancaster, there was no warning at all that they were being followed by a nightfighter. Indeed, navigator Flg Off Charles Clarke only became aware of the aircraft's presence when the port wing was hit and burst into flames. He immediately headed for the escape hatch in the nose, opened it ready for the others to follow him and sat there awaiting the call to bail out, for he knew that the Lancaster had been mortally hit. Shortly thereafter, the port wing broke off, and Clarke dropped out into the darkness. It is thought that the pilot stayed at the controls, the Lancaster crashing between Oberkollwangen and Schmieh, southwest of Calw. Williams and two other crewmen were killed.

Do 217J/Ns appear to have been delivered piecemeal to various operational and training units. The first Do 217J-1 mentioned in Luftwaffe loss records was an aircraft from the *Ergänzungsstaffel* of NJG 2 that suffered an

The most successful Do 217 nightfighter pilot was Hauptmann Rudolf Schoenert. Commencing his nightfighting career in June 1941, he had been credited with 65 aircraft shot down (27 of them in the Do 217) at night and been awarded the *Ritterkreuz mit Eichenlaub* by war's end

accident on 28 May 1942. The first Do 217J-2 loss came on 28 August 1942 when an aircraft from 1./NJG 3 was downed as a result of enemy action. The first Do 217N-1 noted in the loss records was an aircraft that suffered an accident with II./NJG 4 on 11 March 1943. However, five months earlier on 11 October 1942, prototype Do 217N V1 Wk-Nr 1401 had suffered an engine fire during a test flight while with *Erprobungsstaffel*

der Luftwaffe Rechlin. The aircraft crashed into Lake Müritz, and although Feldwebel Günther Ritter and his crew bailed out, they too landed in the lake and drowned. The first Do 217N-2 to be mentioned suffered an accident with 6./NJG 4 on 21 January 1944.

The Italian Regia Aeronautica expressed an interest in acquiring the Do 217 as a nightfighter following Bomber Command raids on northern Italy, and in August 1942 crews began training on the new aircraft. One crew, captained by Tenente Rudolfo Facio, was killed with *Nachtjagdschule* 1 when, on 9 January 1943, their Do 217J-1 crashed west of the airfield at München-Riem.

A total of 12 aircraft were delivered (six J-1s and six J-2s) and operated by 235ª *Squadriglia*, 60° *Gruppo*, 41° *Stormo Intercettori* at Lonate Pozzolo, in northern Italy. 235ª *Squadriglia* was commanded by Capitano Aramis Ammanato, and he was the only pilot to record a victory with the aircraft in Italian service when, on the night of 16 July 1943, he shot down a Lancaster near Vigevano, southwest of Milan. His victim was probably the No 207 Sqn aircraft flown by Plt Off Len Stubbs, which was destroyed during a mission to attack a hydro-electric plant at Cislago, near Milan.

By the end of July, the Italians reported that of the 12 aircraft assigned to 235ª *Squadriglia*, six were unserviceable due to a lack of spares. The last recorded sortie flown by the unit with the Do 217s was on 16 August 1943, after which 235ª *Squadriglia* began converting to the Reggiane Re.2001 Falco II single-seat fighter. In January 1943, Hungary also expressed an interest in acquiring Do 217 nightfighters, but received three Bf 110s instead.

A total of 130 J-1/2s and around 240 N-1/2s (approximately 95 N-1s were converted into N-2s) had been built by the time production ceased in favour of other nightfighter types in October 1943. By then, most operational units had retired their Do 217s, although a number of training and *Nachtaufklärungsstaffeln* and elements of NJGs 4, 100 and 101 continued to operate examples over the Western and Eastern Fronts well into 1944. Indeed, the aircraft's last reported combat loss came on 18 September 1944 when the Do 217N-2 flown by Leutnant Hans-Joachim Beck of *Stab* II./NJG 101 collided with a Soviet Il-4 bomber over the Mátra Forest, 130 km east of Budapest. Both aircraft crashed, resulting in the death of Beck and his crew.

By mid-1943, many of the *Nachtaufklärungsstaffeln* were flying the Do 217. This K-1, which appears to have suffered a collapsed undercarriage while either landing or taxiing, was almost certainly assigned to 4. *Nachtaufklärungsstaffel*. The unit suffered its first Do 217 loss on 30 January 1943 when Do K-1 Wk-Nr 4475 K7+SM failed to return from a mission in the Nowy Oskol–Jelez–Liwny area on the Eastern Front. Oberleutnant Heinz Krickhahn and his crew of three were all reported missing

Do 217K-01 Wk-Nr 4401 KE+JA was part of an initial batch of ten pre-production aircraft that preceded the K-1. It first flew in mid-1942

As well as developing nightfighters, Dornier was also working on a replacement for the Do 217E by January 1942. Designated the Do 217K/M, the 'new' bomber had a totally glazed cockpit to give the crew unhindered all-round vision. Otherwise, however, the Do 217K-1 was essentially a Do 217E-2 with a modified 'stepless' cockpit and BMW 801A engines fitted with a nitrous oxide boost that increased the bomber's speed and range. A shortage of radial engines subsequently meant that the near-identical Do 217M-1 made use of DB 603As instead.

The Do 217K prototype first flew at Rechlin in early July 1942. Do 217M testing was planned to have commenced two months earlier, with the prototype fitted with DB 601A-1 engines. However, the latter were replaced by more powerful DB 603s, and the prototype completed its first flight from Rechlin in September 1942.

A very weathered Do 217M-1, clearly showing the exhaust dampers for night operations. The last two digits on the nose are the Werknummer, which was believed to be 56013, and the fuselage code began RM+. It is thought that this aircraft flew with bomber training unit *Kampfschulgeschwader* 3 at some stage in its career

The night reconnaissance unit 1. *Nachtaufklärungsstaffel*, serving on the Eastern Front, would suffer the new types' first losses when a Do 217K-1 was destroyed in an accident on 6 January 1943, followed by a

Do 217M-1 in another accident on 4 June that same year. From a bomber perspective, it would appear that the first Do 217K-1s reached II./KG 40 in late December 1942/early January 1943, as the first aircraft to suffer an accident was at Soesterberg on 17 January. However, it is not thought that these aircraft were used operationally. IV./KG 2 would also lose a series of Do 217K-1s in training accidents from the end of February.

In September 1943, the Hs 293 was joined in frontline service by the PC 1400X, known as the 'Fritz X'. Both guided bombs were employed operationally by Do 217K-1s and K-2s of III./KG 100

The first example to be destroyed as a result of enemy action appears to have been Unteroffizier Erhard Corty's aircraft from 4./KG 2 that failed to return from an attack on Norwich on the night of 4 May. The first Do 217M-1 loss on operations occurred on the night of 12 June when Hauptmann Otto-Wilhelm Pöhler, *Staffelkapitän* of 1./KG 2 for just under a month, was shot down off Plymouth by Sgt Wilf 'Andy' Miller of Beaufighter-equipped No 125 Sqn.

Another important development for the Do 217 at this time was giving the aircraft the capability to carry and launch remotely controlled glide-bombs. As early as 1939, Henschel had commenced work on such weapons for use against ships. The company's first design was the Hs 293, which entered production in January 1942. This was followed by the Ruhrstahl PC 1400 X, known as 'Fritz X', which was tested from May 1942. The aircraft chosen to launch such missiles were the flawed He 177 and the combat-proven Do 217E.

In April 1942, the first Do 217E-5 (essentially an E-4 modified for Hs 293 operations) arrived at Peenemünde, in northern Germany, for

The larger wing fitted to the Do 217K-2 to allow it to carry the Hs 293 is clearly visible in this view of Wk-Nr 4572, assigned to 5./KG 100. The bomber was one of eight Do 217s destroyed or damaged in an Allied air attack on Kalamaki in Greece on 15 November 1943. It is assumed that the aircraft was abandoned here when the Germans pulled out shortly thereafter. Note the periscope protruding from the top of the cockpit, which meant that this aircraft was fitted with fixed rear-firing guns in the tail

trials aimed at determining its operational range with varying stores configurations. It was hoped that the first missions with the aircraft/ missile combination would subsequently take place over the Atlantic in the spring of 1943. However, political and military interference, a shortage of missiles, unserviceability of both the missiles and aircraft, a paucity of trained aircrew and the decision that after 34 Do 217E-5s had been delivered, a further 107 would be diverted for conventional bombing operations, meant that an in-service date of spring 1943 was no longer possible. Furthermore, it was intended that the He 177 would now become the main launch platform, but with the slipping of the He 177 programme, the Do 217 again became the aircraft of choice in February 1943. The version specifically chosen for the job was the Do 217K-2, with its enlarged wing area capable of carrying two Hs 293 or 'Fritz X' missiles.

With sufficient K-2s available from December 1942, aircraft started to reach Hauptmann Franz Hollweck's II./KG 100 at Garz/Usedorm, followed by Hauptmann Ernst Hetzel's III./KG 100 at Schwäbisch Hall and, later, Giebelstadt. Hollweck had commanded *Versuchsstaffel* 293 from November 1941, the unit subsequently being retitled *Lehr-und Erprobungskommando* 15. Responsible for operational trials with the Hs 293, the unit received its first Do 217E-5s in November 1942 and K-2s shortly thereafter. *Lehr-und Erprobungskommando* 15 was eventually incorporated into II./KG 100.

Hetzel's III./KG 100 had been formed from *Kampfgruppe zur besonderen Verwendung* 21 (subsequently *Lehr-und Erprobungskommando* 21), and its task was to develop the 'Fritz X' into a frontline weapon. Delays with aircraft and missiles persisted, and it was not until 5 July 1943 that the first Do 217E-5s from II./KG 100 moved to Istres, in Southern France, followed a week later by Do 217K-2s from III./KG 100, now commanded by the very experienced Hauptmann Bernhard Jope. The first missions would be flown shortly thereafter.

Do 217E-5 Wk-Nr 5554 of either *Lehr-und Versuchsstaffel* 293 or *Erprobungskommando* 15, which it subsequently became, is carrying a single Hs 293. Note the bulge for the guidance mechanism on the underside of the nose. This aircraft was damaged while serving with I./KG 100 on 13 September 1943, although its subsequent fate is not known

CHAPTER FOUR

MAXIMUM EFFORT, MINIMUM RETURNS

Throughout 1943, the Do 217 would remain active against targets in mainland Britain and shipping both in northwest Europe and, latterly, the Mediterranean, engage RAF heavy bombers as a nightfighter and undertake highly specialised night reconnaissance missions. As the year wore on, the Do 217 would also find itself being gradually replaced by more capable aircraft types, steadily reducing the Dornier's numbers in frontline service.

For the bomber units based in France and the Netherlands, the new year brought a continuation of the campaign against harbours and cities on the east coast of England, as well as mine-laying and 'Pirate' attacks.

The first recorded attack was against Hull, in Yorkshire, on the night of 3 January, resulted in the loss of Unteroffizier Anton Ries and his crew from 9./KG 2 – they were captured after force-landing their battle-damaged E-4 near Spurn Head. The following night saw two mine-laying operations undertaken, with 23 aircraft dropping mines in the Thames Estuary and three inexperienced crews dropping their ordnance off Dungeness, on the Kent coast. Amongst the latter was Unteroffizier Heinz Holzmann and his crew from 4./KG 40, flying their first mission.

Do 217E-4 Wk-Nr 4272 of 9./KG 2 was fitted with the R23 field modification kit that provided a replacement tail cone containing four 7.9 mm MG 81 machine guns in a fixed installation pointing rearwards. The guns were fired electrically from a button on the pilot's control column. The pilot aimed the weapons using a rearward-facing periscope, which can be seen here protruding from the cockpit roof. Wk-Nr 4272 failed to return from a night attack on airfields in Lincolnshire on 15–16 January 1943, by which time it was coded U5+AT. Unteroffizier Hans Unglaube and his crew were all reported missing, having probably been shot down by Flt Lt Joe Singleton of No 25 Sqn

Although the flight went to plan for the Holzmann crew, this was not the case for Feldwebel Hartmut Eucker and his crew, also from 4./KG 40. After taking off from Soesterberg on what would prove to be their first, and last, mission, they crossed the Channel at 6000 ft and headed southwest, dropping to 1000 ft in preparation for releasing their single *Luftmine*. The bomber skimmed the top of a cliff at Fire Hills, bounced several times and then crashed through an empty bungalow at Fairlight, in East Sussex. The Do 217E-4 disintegrated (although the mine did not explode), killing all four crew.

Oberleutnant Karl von Manowarda of 3./KG 2 also participated in this mission, later reporting;

'We had to fly to Margate at 300 m, course 270-280 degrees, 280 km/h, then open the bomb-bay doors and drop the mines. They hung on parachutes. We pilots feared the fuses, as so many different ones were in use. We were happy when we got rid of these beasts. I had just headed for home when our Do 217 was hit. I could not dive as I was only at a height of 300 m, so went high and to port into the pitch dark night. I had no compass, so I kept the constellation of Orion upper left in the canopy window, which led me to the mouth of the River Schelde, where we were ordered to enter Holland. I followed the order precisely, as with a casualty [radio operator Feldwebel Ernst Fröhlich] on board, it was important to find our home base [Gilze-Rijen]. We found it at once, and despite being late and with no radio, landed safely.'

Von Manowarda was commended for completing his mission and bringing back his damaged bomber. His attacker was the Beaufighter flown by Plt Off Ron Densham and his navigator/radar operator Plt Off Henry Ellis of No 29 Sqn. Their combat report read as follows;

'At about 2046 hrs, a contact was obtained level and to starboard about 25 miles northeast of Foreness and controller was informed. The chase continued for 15 minutes on a general northeasterly. The bandit was jinking 30 degrees each side of course at irregular intervals, and losing height slowly and steadily to 400 ft. Beau closed in at 300 mph (270 mph ASI) to 600 ft range, and a Do 217 was identified by exhausts at 400 ft altitude ahead and level.

'Beau gave a two-second burst with all guns at about 150 yards range from dead astern, seeing strikes on port nacelle and port side of fuselage. Inaccurate orange tracer returned from dorsal turret. The port engine of the enemy aircraft caught fire, and enemy aircraft turned rate three, climbing into six-tenths cloud layer from 700 to 1200 ft. Beau followed, but visual contact was lost in cloud with minimum range.'

Von Manowarda would undertake just two more missions with 3./KG 2 (an air-sea rescue mission on 11 January and an attack on a Sunderland two days later) before moving to 11./KG 2 to be an instructor. He would return to operations in October 1943 in command of Ju 188-equipped 1./KG 6 and was shot down and taken prisoner in May 1944.

The Holzmann crew from 4./KG 40 carried out a further seven mine-laying missions and a single attack on Dover during the rest of January. Despite II./KG 40 being kept busy throughout the month, its only loss was the Eucker crew on the 4th.

KG 2, however, would lose two aircraft to nightfighters attacking Lincoln on the night of 15 January. Forty-eight hours later London was bombed for the first time since May 1941, the raid being generated in response to a major attack on Berlin on 16–17 January. A total of 118 aircraft attacked the capital in two waves, their main targets being the King George V and West India Docks and warehouses in the Millwall and Woolwich areas. Although the bombers inflicted serious damage on a power station, nightfighters claimed six aircraft destroyed and three damaged. The only pilot claiming a Do 217 destroyed was Wg Cdr Mike Wight-Boycott of No 29 Sqn, who shot down Unteroffizier Joachim Schnabel's bomber from 7./KG 2. It crashed in Westerham, in Kent, killing all four crew.

There would be just one more Do 217 lost in January when, during a second attack on London on the night of the 20th, this time by just 17 aircraft, a nightfighter flown by either Wg Cdr Bob Braham of No 141 Sqn or Flt Lt Ken Davison of the FIU shot down Feldwebel Leopold Heiden's Do 217E-4 of 4./KG 2 south of Dungeness. German records acknowledge this loss, and that four other aircraft were intercepted by nightfighters and managed to return to base without suffering any damage.

The start of February saw the loss of *Ritterkreuzträger* Oberfeldwebel Karl Müller from 3./KG 2, who was shot down on the night of the 3rd by Flt Lt John Willson of No 219 Sqn while attempting to attack Sunderland. Müller had flown Do 17s on operations with 1./KG 2 from the start of the war, converting to the Do 217 in November 1941. He then remained as an instructor until the following April, when he returned to operations with 1./KG 2. Müller went back to instructing after the Dieppe Raid on 19 August, before joining 3./KG 2 in January 1943 after an apparent disagreement of opinion with his *Kommandeur*, Hauptmann Helmut Powolny. Müller had received the *Deutsches Kreuz* in Gold in June 1942 and the *Ritterkreuz* four months later after completing 280 missions. Willson intercepted Müller's Do 217 just off the Yorkshire coast at Muston, and witnessed it crash on land and saw two crew bail out. No bodies were ever recovered, however.

No fewer than five Do 217s from I. and II./KG 40 were lost between 4 and 8 February, the bombers undertaking mine-laying operations off the Channel coast. All fell victim to either mechanical failure or pilot error.

Between 9 and 12 February, both Do 217 *Geschwader* flew a series of *Störangriff* (nuisance attacks) from as far north as The Wash to as far south as Dartmouth, in Devon, II./KG 40 having moved to Evreux at the start of the month. The Holzmann crew from 4./KG 40 carried out its first *Störangriff* against Woking, in Surrey, on the 9th and Reading, in Berkshire, the following day, the latter attack resulting in the deaths of 41 civilians.

Ritterkreuz recipient Oberfeldwebel Karl Müller of 3./KG 2 was reported missing on 3 February 1943, even though his Do 217E-4, Wk-Nr 5460 U5+GL, crashed on land at Muston, on the North Yorkshire coast, after having been shot down by Flt Lt John Willson of No 219 Sqn

Despite the success of the Reading attack, 10 February was not a good day for II./KG 40. Two aircraft (one of them having targeted Winchester, in Hampshire) returned with wounded crew, while two Do 217s were downed by anti-aircraft fire. Oberleutnant Hans Kleemann of 5./KG 40 was briefed to attack Tangmere, in West Sussex, and he was seen approaching the airfield at 200 ft. A gun battery immediately engaged the aircraft, shooting off the dorsal turret, after which Kleemann attempted a crash-landing at nearby Lagness, only to hit a wall and trees. The bomber disintegrated and the crew was killed. The Do 217 flown by Oberfeldwebel Otto Schneider, also from 5. *Staffel*, was spotted approaching the coast west of Newhaven, in East Sussex, at 500 ft. It too was hit by anti-aircraft fire, shells striking the port wing and causing a fuel tank to explode. The aircraft crashed onto the cliff tops at Saltdean, after which its bomb load exploded.

In these attacks, KG 2 was a little luckier. On 9 February, an aircraft from 2./KG 2 was tasked to attack Hastings, in East Sussex, which it did successfully. However, Flg Off Ron Batten of Spitfire-equipped No 91 Sqn had been scrambled to intercept the bomber. He remembered the weather as being dull and overcast, with a solid cloud base varying between 800 ft and 1200 ft. Batten was directed towards the French coast, and just as he was about to turn for home the Do 217 appeared directly ahead of him, 300-400 ft above and about a mile away;

'It didn't take me long to catch him up. I opened fire at about 25 ft, a short burst on the port engine, then a much longer one moving across the inner wing to the fuselage. Several cannon strikes on the engine and wing could be seen as red flashes, then I had to break off with a sharp turn to starboard to avoid running into him.'

Batten then lost the Do 217 in cloud and carried out an orbit, noticing a line of three parachutes – one of the crew, flight engineer Gefreiter Horst Burkard, stated later that three of the crew bailed out at 200 m, the radio operator having been killed.

Meanwhile, Batten had been told to head for home, but as he crossed the French coast at 700 ft, his engine began to falter and run very roughly. Realising he would not get back over the Channel, Batten closed the throttle, turned to starboard, stuck the nose down and leant forward to switch off the fuel supply. However, he was not able to relock his harness, so when the Spitfire hit the ground near Hardelot, he smashed his head on the gunsight. Batten only came too when, with his Spitfire now on fire, he was pulled out of his cockpit by the crew of a gun battery, one of whom put him over his shoulder and carried him to their nearby headquarters. Batten spent the rest of the war in captivity, while Horst Burkard did not return to operations until the end of April 1943.

The days that followed saw the Do 217s from both *Geschwader* operating from airfields in Normandy attack first Plymouth on the night of 13 February (without any losses) and Swansea three nights later. During the latter mission two aircraft from II./KG 2 were lost to nightfighters from No 125 Sqn, one crew bailed out after becoming lost and another Do 217 suffered engine failure. Finally, the aircraft flown by Feldwebel Friedrich Brandt of II./KG 40 was downed by a Boston intruder of No 605 Sqn, the aircraft crashing at Evreux.

The remainder of February appears to have been much quieter, with mine-laying being the primary focus. I./KG 2 still suffered losses at the hands of the growing nightfighter force, however, with 2. *Staffel* having two Do 217s downed by Wg Cdr Charles Miller of No 29 Sqn on the night of the 26th.

Meanwhile, further east, trials and training by *Lehr-und Erprobungskommando* 15 for employment of the Hs 293 was making slow progress, while a number of *Nachtaufklärungsstaffeln* had converted from the Do 17P to the Do 217E-4 towards the end of 1942, with K-1s arriving in early 1943. By the start of February 1943, all 1. to 4. *Nachtaufklärungsstaffeln* reported operating the Do 217, but exclusively over the Soviet Union. The first combat loss suffered by one of these units, on 29 January, was the Do 217E-4 flown by Oberleutnant Heinz Laubisch of 2. *Nachtaufklärungsstaffel*.

If February had ended quietly, that would all change on the night of 3–4 March, when three waves of bombers attacked London. Amongst the pilots participating in the mission was Feldwebel Günther Vestewig, who had joined 1./KG 2 in October 1942. When he had originally been assigned to I./KG 2, the losses recently suffered by the *Gruppe* had been so heavy that he and his crew were restricted to an intensive training programme for the next four months in an attempt to bring KG 2 back to full operational strength. Three crews were killed in training accidents in December 1942 and were not replaced, which meant that achieving full strength was nigh impossible.

Despite these setbacks, inexperienced pilots like Feldwebel Vestewig soon came to appreciate the flying qualities of the Dornier bomber;

Leutnant Hermann Walther (right) of III./KG 2 inspects damage to one of the propeller blades of his Do 217E-4 at Soesterberg in February 1943. The precise date this incident took place is not known, as the damage was probably too light to warrant it being officially recorded. It is believed that Walther later commanded 16./KG 2, and survived the war

'The Do 217E was a very good aeroplane. Its flying qualities were first class, and without a bombload one could almost fly a full aerobatic sequence with it – loops, rolls left, right, up and down. It only dropped 200 m before one again had full control, and there was no spinning. It also dived very well without airbrakes.'

The Vestewig crew would fly its first mission – mine-laying near Dover – in February 1943, and after another three such sorties it took part in the Swansea attack on 16 February. On 3 March the Vestewig crew would attack London twice. On the first mission, *Gruppenkommandeur* Major Karl Kessel would accompany the crew as observer, the Do 217 (armed with two 500 kg and eight 50 kg bombs) flying from Gilze-Rijen to Ramsgate, in Kent, at low-level. As the aircraft approached London, Vestewig climbed and successfully dropped his bombs south of the Thames. The aircraft duly returned to base on one engine after the other was shut down when it caught fire.

Upon getting back to Gilze-Rijen, Vestewig tried to get some sleep before the second mission of the night. After being awoken by his observer, Obergefreiter Gerhard Polzin, Vestewig's friend Feldwebel Herbert Richter, who had also flown on the first mission, told him that he had a premonition and did not want to fly, but felt duty bound to go. Richter took off ahead of the Vestewig crew, and this time the route flown was via Dover to London. Richter approached the Kent coast on one side of Dover and Vestewig the other, and shortly before making landfall, the latter saw his friend's bomber hit by anti-aircraft fire and crash in flames into the sea.

There were no survivors.

Although no major damage was inflicted on London that night, a tragic accident saw 178 civilians killed and 60 seriously injured when a salvo of defensive rockets panicked people sheltering at Bethnal Green tube station, most of which were then suffocated by the sheer weight of bodies trying to seek cover. KG 2 lost four aircraft to flak with no survivors, while it would appear that Unteroffizier Emil Dansinger's aircraft from 4./KG 2 was possibly shot down by Flt Lt Dick Bennell in a Boston from No 418 Sqn. Although Günther Vestewig was not to know, he would be KG 2's next casualty just four days later.

The target on the night of 7–8 March was Southampton Docks, with aircraft taking off at two-minute intervals. Vestewig and his crew took off at 2258 hrs and headed for Le Havre at 1500 m. They arrived ten minutes early and had to head west, before turning east again back to their mission start point. Climbing in a northerly direction to an altitude of 4000 m, Vestewig headed for Selsey Bill, after which he planned to turn west to attack Southampton. However, Sqn Ldr Geoff Goodman and Flg Off Bill Thomas of No 29 Sqn intervened, chasing the Do 217 for five minutes and watching it jink violently. They then closed to 150 yards and gave the still manoeuvring bomber a three-second burst. Vestewig recalled what happened next;

Feldwebel Günther Vestewig of 1./KG 2 was shot down attacking Southampton on 7–8 March 1943 by Sqn Ldr Geoff Goodman of No 29 Sqn. He bailed out badly wounded, as did his observer Obergefreiter Gerhard Polzin, and survived as a PoW, but the remaining two crewmen were killed

'Suddenly there were sparks in the cockpit, and I heard glass breaking and the intercom stopped working. Between the starboard engine and fuselage I could see flames. Then we could see flames coming from the starboard engine. I turned the aircraft on its nose and dived to extinguish the flames, which got smaller, but when I levelled off, they got bigger than before. I couldn't keep the aeroplane level, and we were now in a left hand downward spiral. There was no chance of reaching the French coast and the danger of explosion was too great. I gave the order to bail out, and my observer cut the radio cable on my helmet. I cannot be certain of what happened next, but my radio operator is buried in Chichester, my flight engineer was reported missing, my observer was wounded by splinters in the nose, chin, left hand and knee and I was seriously wounded with a fractured skull, broken ribs and a bullet through my shin.'

The remains of Oberleutnant Ernst Schneiderbauer's Do 217E-4 Wk-Nr 5441 U5+BL seen at its final resting place near Great Stainton, County Durham, after it had been shot down by Flt Lt John Willson of No 219 Sqn on 11 March 1943. An experienced Fw 200 pilot who had served with I./KG 40 prior to being posted to 3./KG 2, Schneiderbauer bailed out along with the rest of his crew and was captured

The attack proved to be a disaster for KG 2, with the RAF plotting some 30 aircraft 'making landfall between the Isle of Wight and Hastings and having apparently no main objective'. Flt Lt William Hoy and Wg Cdr Vernon Wood of No 604 Sqn each claimed to have destroyed an aircraft, with the Do 217 of Oberfeldwebel Heinz Ahrens from 9./KG 2 coming down south of the Isle of Wight. The other aircraft lost flew into the ground near Octeville, in France, upon returning from the mission.

On the night of 8–9 March, Hull was targeted by KG 2 and Portsmouth attacked by II./KG 40, the latter unit having remained at Evreux. I./KG 2 reported one aircraft from 3. *Staffel* missing and two more lost in accidents, while II./KG 40 had a bomber crash at Saint Aubin, on Jersey, with three crew wounded and one killed. It was Newcastle's turn to be bombed on the nights of 11–12 and 12–13 March, and RAF nightfighters would claim five Do 217s destroyed and two probably destroyed in the defence of the city – KG 2 actually lost two bombers and 6./KG 40 one. Although the crew of the *Stab* III./KG 2 aircraft probably downed by a No 219 Sqn

Beaufighter was lost without trace, Oberleutnant Ernst Schneiderbauer and his crew successfully bailed out of their 3. *Staffel* bomber after it too was attacked over County Durham.

Schneiderbauer had joined I./KG 2 from I./KG 40 in September 1942, the other members of his crew having been transferred in from 6./KG 40 at the same time. His regular observer, Oberfeldwebel Wilhelm Zacharias, had been injured in an accident on 8 February 1943 and duly replaced by the less experienced Unteroffizier Martin Hoffmann. The Schneiderbauer crew had flown many daylight and night missions since then, with Schneiderbauer's personal total standing at around 70 missions over England, and 108 in total.

Flying one of the fastest Do 217s in the *Gruppe* on the night of 11–12 March 1943, the Schneiderbauer crew was tasked with marking the target with flares. Dazzled by searchlights and struggling to pinpoint their exact position, the crew dropped a flare in the hope of spotting a landmark to confirm where they were. Moments later, and with its bomb-bay doors still open, the Dornier was attacked by Flt Lt John Willson of No 219 Sqn, who reported;

'Many strikes were seen on the starboard side of the fuselage in line with the wing and pieces flew off and struck our machine. Enemy aircraft lost height, still turning to starboard, and disappeared immediately. The Nav/Rad then told the pilot there was a burning wreck on the ground below.'

Schneiderbauer recalled;

'Time of the attack was 2325 hrs, and after a low-level flight across the North Sea, at a turning point 50 km south of Newcastle I climbed up to 3300 m. We were northwest of Newcastle when, suddenly, it was like daylight as the pathfinders of II./KG 2 dropped their flares and my radio operator shouted "Nightfighter, coming from the right!" I turned sharply to the right, but a burst from the nightfighter went through the cockpit diagonally. The port windscreen, instrument panel, intercom and port engine were destroyed and the tailplane damaged, so I gave the order to bail out and tried to keep the aeroplane level with the right engine, rudder and by trimming. Meanwhile, the flight engineer tried to open the bottom hatch – I thought it took a long time before he succeeded. He and the radio operator jumped first. I jumped last, just after the observer.'

In the nights that followed, KG 2 would lose six aircraft attacking Sunderland, Grimsby, Norwich and Hartlepool. Things got no better for the *Geschwader* when it targeted Edinburgh alongside Ju 88-equipped KG 6 on the night of 24–25 March. Oberfeldwebel Fritz Kalbfleisch of 3./KG 2 flew into the Cheviot Hills, in Northumberland, while the bombers of Oberleutnant Martin Pischke and Unteroffizier Willi Schneider of 7./KG 2 were apparently damaged by nightfighters before they crashed near Dumfries, in the Scottish borders, and at Haltwhistle, also in Northumberland, respectively. Finally, a fourth Do 217, from 6./KG 2, collided with a radio mast and crashed near Katwijk, on the Dutch coast, killing Unteroffizier Christian Kiechler and his crew.

The losses for the month would end for both *Geschwader* on the night of 28 March when, during an attack on Norwich, Feldwebel Paul Huth of 4./KG 2 and Unteroffizier Hans-Joachim Meinke of 6./KG 40 failed to return, having fallen victim to Flg Off Josef Vopalecky of No 68 Sqn and Flg Off John Beckett of No 157 Sqn, respectively.

March 1943 had been a costly month for the Do 217-equipped units, which would remain heavily tasked following the appointment of Oberstleutnant Dietrich Peltz as *Angriffsführer England* on 24 March. It would be his job to coordinate and intensify the bombing of mainland Britain. KG 2 had suffered the total loss of 25 Do 217s that month, with II./KG 40 losing four. In human terms, 76 crew had been killed or posted as missing and 13 captured from KG 2, with a further 13 killed or missing from II./KG 40. As early as 11 March, captured crews had stated that losses until then had been heavy, few if any replacements had been posted in and many crews had little or no operational experience. This situation would be made worse for KG 2 when, in mid-June 1943, II./KG 40 was withdrawn from operations.

The first Do 217 loss in April came on the night of the 4th when Unteroffizier Martin Hornung's aircraft from 3./KG 2 was damaged by an unidentified nightfighter and ditched 20 km west of Vlissingen. Hornung was the only survivor, being rescued from his dinghy. Unusually, the next loss occurred when Leutnant Walter Held and his crew from I./KG 2 collided with a 'Beaufighter' 15 km northwest of Dreux at 2246 hrs on 9 April while on a training flight from Saint-André-de-l'Eure. At 2202 hrs, Sqn Ldr Hugh Venables of No 418 Sqn had taken off in a Boston from Debden, in Essex, on an intruder mission to the airfields of Melun and Brétigny. He subsequently failed to return. The fact that he and his crew are now buried at Saint-André-de-l'Eure confirms that they had indeed met their fate colliding with Held's Do 217.

Three Dorniers were lost on the night of 11–12 April when two aircraft from 5./KG 2 (including a new Do 217K-1, flown by acting *Staffelführer* Hauptmann Ferdinand Schwankert) and one from 5./KG 40 failed to return from mine-laying. A 3./KG 2 aircraft was downed by a No 400 Sqn Mustang I on the 13th, and the *Geschwader* suffered three more losses in an attack on Chelmsford, in Essex, on the night of 14–15 April, one from 2./KG 2 and two from 6./KG 2.4 and 5./KG 40 also lost Do 217s in the same raid. Four of the bombers fell to Mosquitos from Nos 85 and 157 Sqns.

The threat posed by RAF nightfighters to German bombers was increasing month on month, and the Luftwaffe had tried to combat this by fitting aircraft with Lichtenstein BC/R FuG 214 Gerät rear-warning radar. Units had been instructed in October 1942 that all bombers operating over Britain had to be equipped with Lichtenstein, but the installation of the system had been patchy. For example, by April 1943, only a single Do 217E in 5./KG 40 boasted rear-warning radar, and all the experienced observers serving in the *Staffel* had flown an operational mission in the aircraft in order to familiarise themselves with it. Lichtenstein quickly proved unpopular with crews, as it diverted the observer from his primary duties due to the high levels of concentration required to operate the rear-warning radar.

Oberleutnant Josef Steudel of 8./KG 2 was not convinced of the effectiveness of Lichtenstein;

'There was constant experimenting with the tactics of engagement and technical improvements. One idea was to fit our aircraft with Lichtenstein. This attempt was short-lived, and in my mind not in tune with reality.'

The FuG 101 radio altimeter that also reached frontline Do 217 units at this time proved far more effective, as it allowed crews to fly long distances over the sea at a height of only a few feet. As the nightfighter threat increased, pilots were instructed that the only real way to avoid being intercepted after attacking the target was to fly at 30 ft above the ground – nightfighters rarely descended below 300 ft. The FuG 101 allowed crews to descend to such heights with confidence, as its accuracy was not affected by changes in atmospheric pressure, unlike a normal aneroid altimeter.

The aircraft downed during the Chelmsford raid would be the last losses in April due to operations subsequently continuing at a much reduced tempo. Amongst the handful of missions flown was an attack on Aberdeen on the night of 21 April, for which 30 aircraft from I. and II./KG 2 and an unknown number from II./KG 40 had flown to Stavanger, in Norway, the day before. The attack by 29 Do 217s was successful, with 127 bombs dropped on and around the city, killing 98 civilians and 27 soldiers – the latter had died when their barracks suffered a direct hit. Although no aircraft were lost on the raid itself, during the return flight to the Netherlands on 25 April, Feldwebel Günther Stahr and his crew from 4./KG 2 perished following a collision with an escorting Fw 190 flown by Unteroffizier Hermann Gagla of 1./JG 11.

Compared to the previous month, April 1943 had been far less costly in terms of aircraft destroyed (eight from KG 2 and three for II./KG 40) and aircrew lost (32 killed and three captured from KG 2 and nine killed and three captured from II./KG 40).

May would start badly for KG 2, and it would be the last full month of Do 217 operations for II./KG 40. It also saw the first accidents suffered by

On 4 May 1943, Leutnant Ernst Andres crash-landed Do 217K-1 Wk-Nr 4415 U5+AA of *Stab.*/KG 2 near Amsterdam after the bomber developed engine problems whilst returning from an attack on Norwich. Three of the crew were badly injured and *Geschwaderkommodore* Major Ernst Bradel and a gunner were killed. This photograph of the funeral cortège shows that Bradel was buried with full military honours

Do 217K-2s of III./KG 100 and the continued existence, for the time being, of Do 217E-5-equipped *Lehr-und Erprobungskommando* 15. The various *Nachtjagd* units (namely NJGs 3 and 4) suffered a number of accidents but no combat losses. One final, unusual, loss for the theatre was the Do 217K-1 of *Flugbereitschaft/ Luftflottenkommando* 2 flown by Oberfeldwebel Sieghart Glashagel, which went missing on a flight between Rome and Tunis. Its loss was attributed to Allied fighters but no claims match, even remotely. However, Unteroffizier Hans-Wilhelm Ellmers of 1./JG 53 claimed the destruction of a B-25, and none of this type were lost or damaged on the date in question.

After a few nights of mining, the first major attack of May 1943 was mounted against Norwich by 43 Do 217s and 36 Ju 88s on the night of the 4th. Although the city was hit, Unteroffizier Georg Hägler of 2./KG 2 was shot down near Eindhoven, in the Netherlands, by the Mosquito nightfighter flown by Flg Off Brian Williams of No. 605 Sqn, and the aircraft of Oberfeldwebel Heinrich Meyer of 6./KG 2 was shot down near Hilversum, also in the Netherlands – his assailant was unknown. The previously mentioned Do 217K-1 of Unteroffizier Erhard Corty also failed to return. A fourth aircraft, flown by Leutnant Ernst Andres of *Stab*./KG 2 was lost in an accident when it developed engine problems and crash-landed at Lansdmeer, near Amsterdam. One of two Do 217K-1s destroyed that night, its crew of five included the *Geschwaderkommodore*, Major Walter Bradel. Three of the crew were badly injured, while Bradel, who had not strapped himself in, and the gunner were killed.

Ritterkreuz recipient Bradel was a serious loss to KG 2 at such a critical time. He had flown in Spain during the Civil War and seen action in Ju 52/3ms during the invasion of Norway in 1940, before moving to KG 2 in September of that year to take command of 9. *Staffel*. In December 1941, by which time he had been awarded the *Ritterkreuz*, Bradel took command of II./KG 2. He had been promoted to *Geschwaderkommodore* at the end of January 1943. Bradel would be replaced by Major Karl Kessel, formerly *Gruppenkommandeur* of I./KG 2.

Following the Norwich raid, it would appear that both KG 2 and II./KG 40 went back to mine-laying, for the next casualties occurred while undertaking this often hazardous operation on 11 May. Leutnant Eberhard Pleiss of 3./KG 2 was apparently blinded by searchlights and crashed into the sea off Lowestoft at 2323 hrs, while Leutnant Hans-Joachim Wolf of 6./KG 40 failed to return to Gilze-Rijen that same night. On 13–14 May KG 2 carried out another major attack on Chelmsford, and this resulted in the loss of single Do 217s from 2., 4. and 6./KG 2. Two of the bombers were credited to No 85 Sqn crews, with the third Do 217 probably falling victim to anti-aircraft fire. Indeed, returning crews noted that the target area was well defended by 'Flak', and several 'Flak' ships were also encountered off the Essex coast.

Two nights later, an attack on Sunderland resulted in the loss of a Do 217K-1 flown by Unteroffizier Karl Roos of 6./KG 2, the bomber being attacked by Flg Off Brian Keele of No 604 Sqn. That same night a Do 217E-4 of II./KG 40 collided with an obstacle and crashed in flames at Groet, killing all four crew.

During the afternoon of 17 May, I./KG 2 moved to Rennes (losing a Do 217 in an accident en route) and II./KG 2 to Vannes, and that night

Do 217E-4 Wk-Nr 5424 F8+CM of 4./KG 40 breaks away from another Dornier during a training mission in early May 1943. This aircraft failed to return from a mission on 18 May 1943, Oberfeldwebel Erich Harms and his crew being reported missing. Wk-Nr 5424 was II./KG 40's penultimate operational Do 217 loss prior to the *Gruppe* converting to the Me 410 and being redesignated V./KG 2

both units – along with II./KG 40 and Ju 88-equipped KG 6 – attacked Cardiff. Although nightfighters were reported, there were no claims for Do 217s destroyed, despite KG 2 losing two bombers. To make matters worse a K-1 became lost and crashed near Grand-Champs, in Brittany, at 0615 hrs after it ran out of fuel on the return leg of the mission. Only one crewman survived. The final loss of the night was the 2./KG 2 aircraft flown by Leutnant Wilhelm Polzer, which crashed at Romazy, 80 km northeast of Rennes, killing all four crew.

The night of 23–24 May would see the last major attack of the month, and the final ever raid undertaken by Do 217s of II./KG 40 prior to the *Gruppe* converting to the Me 410 and being redesignated V./KG 2. The crew of Unteroffizier Heinz Holzmann of 4./KG 40 recorded their 29th operational flight since 4 January 1943, taking off from Gilze-Rijen at 0040 hrs to attack Sunderland and landing at 0446 hrs after having dropped two SC 500 and four SC 50 bombs, and two AB 500 incendiary bomb containers, on the city. The aircraft flown by Oberfeldwebel Herbert Mitzscherling of 1./KG 2 and Leutnant Friedrich Weiss of 5./KG 40 failed to return, with Sqn Ldr George Bower of No 409 Sqn making the only nightfighter claim off the coast from South Shields.

The only other Do 217-equipped unit to report a loss in May 1943 was II./KG 100, which had an E-5 written off. The recording of this incident serves as proof that *Lehr-und Erprobungskommando* 15 had now been fully absorbed into the new unit, which was still not operational with the Hs 293. Although there were no nightfighters destroyed on operations, a few Do 217J-1s and N-1s of 4./NJG 1, 5./NJG 3 and I./NJG 4 suffered damage in accidents.

June 1943 would be a quieter month for KG 2, now the only operational Do 217 unit on the Western Front. It would suffer just three losses in combat this month – the E-4 of Oberleutnant Karl-Heinz Göllner of 3./KG 2 during a raid on London on the night of the 5th, the M-1 of Hauptmann Otto-Wilhelm Pöhler, *Staffelkapitän* of 1./KG 2, in an attack on Plymouth on 12–13 June, and the E-4 of Feldwebel Friedrich Sünnemann of 5./KG 2 when Grimsby was bombed the following night. The latter two bombers fell victim to nightfighters, Pöhler to Sgt Wilf Miller of No 125 Sqn and Sünnemann to Flg Off David Wills of No 68 Sqn (who, that night, was flying with No 604 Sqn).

Pöhler was another loss that hit KG 2 particularly hard. He had flown with 6./KG 55 in the Battle of France until he was shot down and taken prisoner on 13 May 1940. Once freed following the capitulation of France, Pöhler joined II./KG 40, before taking command of 9./KG 2 at the end of January 1943. Made *Geschwader* technical officer in mid-April, he had been *Staffelkapitän* of 1./KG 2 for less than a month when he was killed.

June also saw the first loss for recently formed 1./KG 66, which had taken over pathfinder duties from 15./KG 6 at Chartres in April. The latter unit could trace its origins to *Lehr-und Erprobungskommando* 17 and *Lehr-und Erprobungskommando* 100 (also known as *Lehr-und Erprobungskommando XY*). Although not yet fully operational, 1./KG 66 suffered its first casualties at 0040 hrs on 21 June when Unteroffizier Kurt Winter and his four crew were killed in the crash of their Do 217K-1 at Saint-Georges-du-Mesnil, near Montdidier, after it was probably shot down by a Boston flown by Flt Lt Massy Beveridge of No 418 Sqn.

Other losses in June were as a result of accidents, rather than combat, to the various *Nachtaufklärungsstaffel* on the Eastern Front and to II. and III./KG 100, which was still training for Hs 293 operations. Nightfighter attrition was also very light, and again all due to accidents. One notable loss was to the *Einsatzstaffel* of II./KG 101, the latter having

A Do 217E-4 of I./KG 66 seen at Chartres. Note the large X Gerät aerial above the cockpit. This specialist pathfinding unit evolved from *Eprobungskommando XY* via *Lehr-und Erprobungskommando* 100, *Lehr-und Erprobungskommando* 17 and 15./KG 6, before it was finally designated I./KG 66 in April 1943. The Do 217 proved to be unsuited to this demanding role

been formed in February 1943 from *Kampfschulgeschwader* 1. Tasked with carrying out trials and bombing evaluation, the *Einsatzstaffel* had moved from Greifswald, in northeastern Germany, to Pskov-South, on the Lithuania–Russia border, in May 1943 for the operational evaluation of the Do 217 as a high-altitude bomber. On 8 June Leutnant Eduard Steyrer's E-4 was shot down by Soviet anti-aircraft fire near Volkhov.

July would see a significant increase in losses for KG 2, with 18 Do 217s lost in combat or accidents, 57 crew killed and two captured. Targets remained the same as in previous months, with London, Grimsby and Hull all being bombed and a handful of mine-laying missions being completed. Daylight raids were also undertaken, however, with the first of these being performed on 9 July. Making the most of a spell of poor weather, eight Do 217s carried out a daring low-level attack south of London.

Four aircraft attacked houses while the observer in another Do 217 reported dropping two 500 kg and 12 50 kg bombs on an army convoy in what he thought was Tunbridge Wells, in Kent, at 1721 hrs. The aircraft had, in fact, dropped its ordnance on East Grinstead, in West Sussex, eight bombs detonating in London Road and the High Street with deadly effect. Among the buildings hit was the Whitehall Cinema on London Road, which was full at the time. The roof collapsed, killing many of the audience. A total of 108 people died that day and a further 235 were injured.

Two of the attackers failed to return. Leutnant Hans-Hellmut Dunzelt of 5./KG 2 made the mistake of flying at just 300 ft directly over Kenley airfield, where the ground defences opened fire. The bomber was duly hit and crashed at nearby Bletchingly at 1727 hrs. At exactly the same time, Oberleutnant Hermann Zink's Do 217K-1 of 6./KG 2 dived into the ground at Bicknor, in Kent. Almost simultaneously, a Mosquito of No 85 Sqn crewed by Flt Lt John Lintott and Plt Off George Gillings-Lax crashed at Boxley, near Maidstone in Kent. Part of the report into their combat read as follows;

'The GCI controller reports that at 1719 hrs, Flt Lt Lintott was put onto a raid at 6000 ft travelling on 020 degrees, and that a contact was obtained at 1724 hrs and held. At 1727 hrs, both blips, which were merged, ended, and it was thought that this was due to both aircraft losing height rapidly.'

All ten aircrew (eight German and two British) were killed in these engagements.

Aside from the threat posed by nightfighters over British targets, bomber crews from KG 2 were now also having to deal with an increasing number of Allied intruders – by both night and day – causing problems over their airfields in France. For example, on 12 July, Flt Lt Duncan Grant of Mustang I-equipped No 400 Sqn shot down the Do 217M-1 flown by 9. *Staffel*'s Unteroffizier Friedrich Nieberlein 12 miles northeast of Chartres at 1710 hrs. Grant's combat report stated;

'While flying at zero feet in the area north of Chartres, two Do 217s were seen at 1500 ft flying line astern about three miles apart. The Mustang passed underneath rear aeroplane, did a tight turn towards aircraft and came in line astern at zero feet. When about 100 yards behind and underneath, he climbed up to dead astern at 400 yards. Flt Lt Grant opened with intermittent bursts for ten seconds. Saw strikes all over fuselage and both engines began smoking. After closing to 100 yards, port engine blew up with bright orange flames. Broke off attack and saw crew bail out. Aircraft started to turn to port, losing height to 100 ft, where it rolled over on back and was seen to crash into ground and burst into flames.'

Two crew were wounded and Nieberlein was killed.

Meanwhile, in the Mediterranean, II. and III./KG 100 were at last preparing for operations. On 5 July the first Do 217E-5s from Hauptmann Franz Hollweck's II./KG 100 had moved to Istres, in southern France, to commence Hs 293 operations, although shortly thereafter the aircraft moved to Cognac on France's Atlantic coast. A week later, Do 217K-2s from Hauptmann Bernhard Jope's III./KG 100 flew in to Istres, having been declared mission-ready with the PC 1400 X. A *Kette* then moved to Foggia, in Italy, on 17 July, and four days later the unit mounted an ineffective attack on Allied shipping between Augusta and Sicily on the evening of the 21st. Successes for both units would soon come during the next two months, however.

Combat losses of Do 217 nightfighters had been very rare until the night of 15 July, when two were lost from 5./NJG 4. Feldwebel Helmut Späte

had just shot down his first aircraft (a Halifax of No 10 Sqn flown by Sgt Harry Mellor) when his Do 217N-1 was hit by return fire from a second aircraft, causing him to crash at Voisin. Späte and one other crewman were killed. The second loss was more spectacular, Unteroffizier Heinrich Prinz colliding with a No 10 Sqn Halifax flown by Flt Sgt Bill Pyle. The RAF bomber crashed into Besançon railway station, killing the crew, while the Do 217N-1 came down at La Barre. The crew of the Dornier also perished.

August 1943 would be notable for two major night raids on Portsmouth on the 15th and Lincoln on the 17th. Both attacks caused only slight damage, and the Portsmouth operation cost KG 2 six Do 217s (all bar one of them M-1s), with the deaths off 27 aircrew. A seventh bomber, flown by Hauptmann Albert Schreiweis, *Gruppenkommandeur* of III./KG 2, had one of its engines destroyed by anti-aircraft fire. Schreiweis crash-landed in a cornfield near Evreux, injuring all four crew.

The Lincoln attack cost KG 2 another eight aircraft, resulting in 24 aircrew being killed and five captured. Three more aircraft were damaged, with nine more aircrew being injured or wounded. Mosquito nightfighters from Nos 256 and 410 Sqns claimed four Do 217s destroyed during the Portsmouth attack, with one more probably destroyed and one damaged, while Beaufighter-equipped Nos 68 and 604 Sqns claimed to have destroyed five Dorniers during the Lincoln raid, with three more probably destroyed.

The Lincoln mission also saw 1./KG 66 suffer its second combat loss when the Do 217E-4 flown by Oberfeldwebel Ernst Stemplinger failed to return. No further Dorniers were lost in combat by KG 2 or I./KG 66 for the remainder of the month, attacks by the Me 410s of V./KG 2 being preferred following the high attrition suffered by the Do 217s over Portsmouth and Lincoln.

August 1943 also saw the first successful attack made by II./KG 100 using Hs 293s when, on the 25th, 12 Do 217E-5s led by *Geschwaderkommodore* Major Fritz Aufhammer and escorted by seven Ju 88C-6s from V./KG 40 attacked a convoy in the Bay of Biscay, damaging the frigate HMS *Waveney* and the sloops HMS *Bideford* and HMS *Landguard*. Able Seaman Charles

Do 217M-1 Wk-Nr 722852 U5+ET of 9./KG 2 was destroyed during a raid on Portsmouth on 15–16 August 1943 when Leutnant Theo Bach lost control of the bomber while being held by a searchlight. The aircraft crashed at Horndean, in Hampshire, killing all four crew

The 1200-ton sloop HMS *Egret* has the unfortunate distinction of being the first ship to be sunk by an air-launched guided missile, the vessel being hit 30 nautical miles west of the Spanish coastal city of Vigo on 27 August 1943. Credit for its sinking was given to Major Fritz Aufhammer of 5./KG 100

Boardman was the only fatality, the sailor being killed when *Bideford* was hit by an Hs 293 that failed to explode.

The following day, Ju 88Cs from 15./KG 40 went looking for more targets for II./KG 100 and duly discovered six warships from the 1st Support Group searching for U-boats. At 1415 hrs on 27 August, 14 Do 217s, together with their escorts, approached the warships, which were 30 nautical miles west of the Spanish coastal city of Vigo. Dividing into three groups, seven Hs 293s targeted the sloop HMS *Egret*, commanded by Lt Cdr John Waterhouse. One bomb was shot down, five fell short but the last one hit the warship's munitions stores, which exploded. No fewer than 194 sailors, plus four RAF Y-Service electronics specialists who were monitoring German aircraft radio traffic, were killed, with 35 survivors being rescued by the Canadian destroyer HMCS *Athabaskan*. The latter was then targeted, the destroyer suffering heavy damage and the deaths of three crew when an Hs 293 passed through *Athabaskan* prior to detonating outside of the ship.

The sinking of *Egret* was credited to Major Aufhammer and Oberleutnant Otto Paulus, while the damage to *Athabaskan* was caused by Hauptmann Wolfgang Vorpahl of 5./KG 100. As a result of these attacks, anti-U-boat operations by Allied warships in the Bay of Biscay were temporarily suspended.

Although II./KG 100 suffered no losses in the two attacks, that same month III./KG 100 lost Do 217K-2s from 8. *Staffel* (flown by Leutnant Robert Bürkle) and 9. *Staffel* (flown by Unteroffizier Silvio Schenck) attacking Palermo, on Sicily, on 1 August. On the 10th, an aircraft from *Stab* III./KG 100 flown by Leutnant Hans-Joachim Zantopp was shot down 30 km north of Milazzo, again on Sicily, by a Beaufighter of No 108 Sqn flown by Plt Off Bill Henderson. Zantopp and one other crewman were picked up by a Walrus of No 283 Sqn.

Over Britain, September 1943 would be the quietest month for the Luftwaffe's bomber force since the start of the war. KG 2 recorded the loss of just two aircraft on mine-laying operations, although two more Do 217s from 7. *Staffel* collided over the North Sea on 22 September. Amongst the aircrew seeing little in the way of action this month were Unteroffizier Jakob Burkhard of 2./KG 2, who flew just one mine-laying mission on the 22nd, and Oberleutnant Josef Steudel, now *Staffelkapitän* of 8./KG 2, who completed two such missions on 3 and 7 September.

Meanwhile, in the Mediterranean, things were much busier for Do 217 crews in the wake of the Operation *Avalanche* landings at Salerno, on the southwest coast of Italy, which commenced on 3 September. The Italian surrender five days later proved fortuitous for the Allies, as the principal warships of the Regia Marina should have been attacking the landings. Instead, on 9 September, a 17-strong fleet, which included the battleships *Roma*, *Vittoria Veneto* and *Italia*, set sail from La Spezia to prevent the vessels falling into German hands. When the Italian intentions became known, the Luftwaffe sent III./KG 100 to attack them with '*Fritz X*' guided bombs.

So far that month, just one Do 217K-2 had been lost – the *Stab* III./KG 100 aircraft flown by Feldwebel Karl Schwartz on 5 September. Now, III./KG 100 shadowed the fleet until it reached the Strait of Bonifacio, between Corsica and Sardinia, at which point 11 aircraft attacked from 1537 hrs.

Major Bernhard Jope led the first '*Fritz X*' unit, III./KG 100, before taking overall command of KG 100 in September 1943. This photograph was taken in 1944, after he had been awarded the *Ritterkreuz mit Eichenlaub*

It is believed that the first strike was led by Major Bernhard Jope, whose observer, Unteroffizier Lori Klapproth, achieved a near miss that temporarily jammed *Roma*'s rudder. A second attack wave, led by Oberleutnant Heinrich Schmetz, saw Unteroffizier Heinrich Penz, observer to Leutnant Klaus Deumling of 7./KG 100 who was on his first mission, hit *Roma* on the starboard side. Photographic evidence exists of the attack by Unteroffizier Eugen Degan, the observer in Oberfeldwebel Kurt Steinborn's Do 217K-1 of 7./KG 100, who also reported hitting *Roma* on the starboard side. At the same time, *Roma*'s sister-ship *Italia* was attacked.

The second glide-bomb to hit *Roma* passed through the ship and exploded under its keel. Water now flooded the engine and boiler rooms and numerous electrical fires broke out throughout the vessel. Losing speed, *Roma* began lagging behind, and at 1602 hrs another '*Fritz X*' from a second wave of seven Do 217s detonated in the forward engine room. More flames and flooding ensued, followed by an explosion in the magazine of the No 2 main turret. This caused even more flooding, after which *Roma* began sinking bow first until it capsized and broke in two. At least 1253 sailors went down with the ship, with a further 593 men being rescued.

Italia enjoyed better luck, as the '*Fritz X*' that hit it forward of the No 1 main turret passed through the ship and exited the hull, before exploding in the water beneath the vessel. Although the latter was holed, letting in 1060 tons of water, the battleship managed to limp into Malta harbour.

By now II./KG 100 and its Hs 293-equipped Do 217s had rejoined III./KG 100 in the Mediterranean. The Dornier's next success came at 1000 hrs on 11 September when a single 'Fritz X' passed through the roof of 'C' turret on board the light cruiser USS *Savannah* (CL-42), killing 36 crew in the turret and a damage control party when the glide-bomb exploded in the lower ammunition handling room. The blast tore a large hole in the ship's hull, opened a seam in its side and blew out all fires in the boiler rooms. *Savannah* now lay dead in the water with its forecastle nearly awash, and eight hours elapsed before the boilers were relit so that the ship could get underway for Malta. A total of 197 crew were killed and 15 seriously wounded. Four more were trapped in a watertight compartment, and were not rescued until after *Savannah* had docked in Malta on the 12th.

The light cruiser HMS *Uganda* was then hit by a bomb off Salerno at 1440 hrs on 13 September, the weapon passing through seven decks and straight through its keel before exploding underwater just beneath the hull. The concussive shock of the detonation extinguished all of the cruiser's boiler fires, 1300 tons of water was taken on through the hole in the keel and 16 sailors were killed. *Uganda* had to be towed to Malta for repairs. Three aircraft were lost to Spitfires of Nos 81 and 111 Sqns on the 13th, although Oberleutnant Erwin Burghoff and his crew from *Stab* III./KG 100 claimed to have shot one of their attackers down before they bailed out of their stricken Do 217 over German-held territory. The Spitfire of Plt Off Bill Fell from No 81 Sqn was indeed hit by return fire, forcing him to also bail out over enemy territory. He subsequently managed to evade capture.

At least two merchant ships were probably hit by either Hs 293s or 'Fritz Xs' off Salerno on 14 September, with two Do 217s from III./KG 100 attacking vessels in the same location the following day – one crew claimed to have sunk an 8000-ton freighter with a single 'Fritz X'. Then, on 16 September, III./KG 100 came very close to achieving yet another spectacular success with 'Fritz X' when a weapon hit the battleship HMS *Warspite* while it was providing gunfire support at Salerno. One glide-bomb penetrated six decks before exploding in the No. 4 boiler room, putting out all fires and blowing a 20-ft hole in its double hull. A second 'Fritz X' near-missed *Warspite*, holing the torpedo bulges at the waterline that then took on 5000 tons of water. A third weapon missed completely. Having lost steam and, consequently all power, the battleship had to be taken under tow.

The first hit was by a missile launched from the Do 217K-2 flown by Oberleutnant Heinrich Schmetz of 9./KG 100, his observer being Unteroffizier Oskar Huhn, with the remaining two glide-bombs being directed by Feldwebel Meyer and Obergefreiter Mrzowitzki.

The 45,500-ton battleship *Roma* of the *Regia Marina* was easily the largest vessel sunk by the 'Fritz X', the warship being hit by two guided bombs dropped by III./KG 100 on 9 September 1943 as its sailed through the Strait of Bonifacio

Although the damage inflicted on *Warspite* had been considerable, casualties amounted to only nine killed and 14 wounded. Towed by a cruiser and four destroyers to Malta, where emergency repairs were carried out, the battleship was then towed to Gibraltar, before returning to Britain under its own steam in March 1944. Subsequently out of action for nearly nine months, *Warspite* – a survivor of the Battle of Jutland in World War 1 – was never completely repaired. Nevertheless, it participated in the bombardment of German positions in Normandy on 6 June 1944.

The last *'Fritz X'* attack at Salerno damaged the light cruiser USS *Philadelphia* (CL-41) with two near misses on 17 September – the same day III./KG 100 flew its last *'Fritz X'* mission over the beachhead.

Seven Do 217E-5s and three Do 217K-2s were lost by II. and III./KG 100 between 13 and 17 September. Both *Gruppen* would remain in southern France until mid-November 1943, losing another four Do 217E-5s and the first Do 217K-3 on operations and in accidents. One of those killed in action during this period was the newly appointed *Gruppenkommandeur* of II./KG 100, Hauptmann Heinz Molinnus, who was killed on 4 October when his E-5 crashed on landing at Istres after attacking Allied ships. II./KG 100 suffered three losses on 30 September when attacking shipping supporting the landings at Ajaccio, on Corsica, Hs 293s dropped by the *Gruppe* damaging the French destroyer *Le Fortuné* and sinking the landing ship HM LST-79, which was carrying LCT-2231. French Spitfires of *Groupe de Chasse* 2/7 were credited with downing the three Do 217s.

Hauptmann Wolfgang Vorpahl's 5./KG 100 had moved to Kalamaki, in Greece, in late October, from where it carried out Hs 293 operations in the Aegean Sea. The *Staffel* badly damaged the escort destroyer HMS *Rockwood* (it was later declared a total destructive loss, despite the Hs 293 failing to explode) and sunk the destroyer HMS *Dulverton* on 11 and 13 November, respectively. However, on 15 November, 5. *Staffel* had eight aircraft destroyed or badly damaged in an air attack on Kalamaki, after which the surviving Do 217s rejoined II./KG 100 at Toulouse-Blagnac in mid-December.

In northwest Europe, changes were afoot for the dwindling number of Do 217-equipped units. In October 1943, II./KG 2 began converting to the Ju 188E-1, leaving the remaining two *Gruppen* flying a mixed fleet of Do 217E-4s, K-1s and M-1s. As had been the case the previous month, losses continued to be light in October. Just three bombers were destroyed, the first being the Do 217M-1 flown by Oberfeldwebel Paul Treiber of 3./KG 2 that was claimed by Plt Off Jan Serhant of No 68 Sqn off the East Anglian coast on the 7th. The remaining two aircraft were both lost without trace during an attack on Great Yarmouth on the night of the 23rd, the Do 217M-1 flown by Leutnant Wolf Müller of 7./KG 2 and the Do 217K-1 of Hauptmann Max Pommerening, *Staffelkapitän* of 9./KG 2, probably

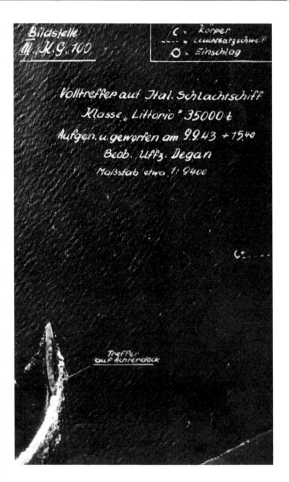

Photographic evidence of Unteroffizier Eugen Degan's successful attack on *Roma* at 1540 hrs 9 September 1943. The battleship has already been hit once, and is about to be struck a second time

falling to anti-aircraft fire. Oberleutnant Josef Steudel of 8./KG 2 reported strong defences from light and heavy guns during this raid, and he also spotted three nightfighters, although no RAF claims were filed that night.

Losses by other Do 217 combat units in October 1943 appear to have been limited to those flying nightfighters, with 5./NJG 3 losing a Do 217N-1 on the 18th when the aircraft of Hauptmann Paul Szameitat was hit in both engines by a Lancaster of No 101 Sqn flown by Sgt Ron Daye that subsequently crashed at Weetzen, in Germany. The crew of the Dornier bailed out and the aircraft crashed at Barsinghausen. 4. and 6./NJG 101 lost a Do 217N-1 and J-1, respectively, on 22 October. Finally, 3./NJG 100 experienced its first loss over the Eastern Front the following night when the Do 217J-1 flown by Feldwebel Walter Schienbein suffered engine failure and crashed near Toltoschina. Although the pilot and one other crewman survived with injuries, two were killed.

November would be even quieter for I. and III./KG 2, with the only loss being a Do 217K-1 from 9./KG 2 during a night raid by seven Dorniers on Norwich on the 6th. The pilot, Leutnant Gerhard Wulfhorst, was apparently incapacitated by a shell splinter, lost control and crashed at Gillingham, in Norfolk. The radio operator, Unteroffizier Alwin Körk, bailed out and was the only survivor. He landed near the burning wreckage of his aeroplane, which was then attacked by another Do 217 – one bomb exploded just 40 yards from Körk!

Both Oberleutnant Josef Steudel of 8./KG 2 and Unteroffizier Jakob Burkardt of 2./KG 2 each flew just one mission that month, attacking Ipswich on 3 November.

The only other combat loss in November was a Do 217N-1 of *Stab* II./NJG 101, which crashed due to enemy action on 26 November, killing Oberleutnant Alfred Günther and two crew.

December started badly for KG 2 when, on the 4th, Typhoons from Nos 198 and 609 Sqns attacked Eindhoven and Gilze-Rijen airfields –

These Do 217K-2s of 7./KG 100 were almost certainly photographed at Istres, near Marseilles, in August–September 1943

No 198 Sqn claimed to have destroyed four Do 217s and No 609 Sqn seven. Five Dorniers were in fact lost and one damaged, four of the aircraft written off and the one damaged bomber coming from 3. *Staffel*, with the other Do 217 destroyed being a 7. *Staffel* machine. Eleven aircrew were killed and nine wounded. The only other losses occurred on the night of 10 December when, during an attack on Chelmsford, a M-1 of *Stab.*/KG 2, two M-1s from 2./KG 2 and a K-1 of 8./KG 2 were lost. Flg Off Rayne Schultz of No 410 Sqn claimed three of the bombers destroyed and the fourth was credited to Wg Cdr Dennis Hayley-Bell, CO of No 68 Sqn.

1943 had been the toughest year so far for Do 217 crews, who suffered heavy losses, but at the same time achieved a number of notable successes. However, newer aircraft were starting to replace the Dornier, with II./KG 2 swapping to the superior Ju 188 and I./KG 66 finding the Ju 88S to be far better in the pathfinding role than the Do 217. Furthermore, nightfighter pilots felt that the Do 217J did not meet their exacting requirements, and although the lighter but more heavily armed N-model was an improvement, most aviators still considered this aircraft to be a poor stopgap measure. A good rate of climb and manoeuvrability – essential in a fighter – were present, but only just. Only a minority of pilots, including Hauptmann Rudolf Schoenert, considered the Do 217 to be a useful nightfighter. As a result, it too began to diminish in numbers, and by August 1944, the Do 217 as a combat aircraft had all but disappeared.

A close-up of the FuG 202 Lichtenstein radar dipole antenna array and four MG 151 20 mm cannon and two MG 81 7.7 mm machine gun armament installed in the nose of a Do 217N-1. Despite the last three digits of the Werknummer being displayed on the nose of the aircraft, its career and fate remain unknown

CHAPTER FIVE

DECLINE AND DISAPPEARANCE

Do 217M-1 Wk-Nr 56125 U5+UK of 2./KG 2 suffered an accident at Eindhoven on 7 September 1943, and after being repaired it was assigned to 9./KG 2 as U5+CT. On 20–21 April 1944, the bomber was lost attacking Hull, probably being shot down by Flg Off Harry White of No 141 Sqn. Obergefreiter Hermann Went and his crew were all killed when the aircraft crashed into the North Sea. The significance of the large number '2' on the tail has never been properly explained

On 7 December 1943, Dr Josef Goebbels, the Reich Minister for Propaganda, wrote;

'Göring has now gone west to prepare the reprisal attacks against England. For this we need about 200 heavy four-engined aircraft which will in one night fly to England twice and deliver a massive blow against the capital. Of course, we cannot carry out an attack like this often enough, but it should serve as a reminder to the English that we are still around.'

This optimistic outburst resulted from a conference held at the end of the previous month in which Reichsmarschall Hermann Göring had decreed that a major bombing campaign against London, codenamed Operation *Steinbock*, would commence in two weeks' time. In reality, it was not until the night of 21 January 1944 that the first major attack was launched.

The British were aware that something was afoot when signal intercepts revealed the movement of Luftwaffe bomber units from Italy to bases in France and Belgium. Further activity at German airfields during the afternoon of 21 January 1944 clearly showed that *Steinbock*, or the 'Baby Blitz' as it became known, was about to start.

Prior to this date, the only Do 217 losses in northwest Europe occurred on 4 January as a result of a return visit to Gilze-Rijen by Typhoons from Nos 198 and 609 Sqns. Flying a series of strafing passes, No 198 Sqn claimed the destruction of one Do 217 and No 609 Sqn claimed four. KG 2 reported the loss of four aircraft, with several more being damaged. Four aircrew were killed, including Oberleutnant Otto Schäfer, *Staffelkapitän* of 7./KG 2, and five wounded.

The Luftwaffe had 35 Do 217s, 20 Me 410s, 20 Fw 190s, 30 He 177s and 170 Ju 88/188s available for the first night of *Steinbock*. Two waves of attacks were flown and an incredible 16 Ju 88s, two Ju 188s, eight He 177s, one Fw 190, one Me 410 and four Do 217s (from I. and III./KG 2) were lost either to British defences or in crashes flying to or from the target. The only claim for a Do 217 was filed by Flt Lt John Hall of Mosquito-equipped No 488 Sqn during the first wave. This was probably the M-1 of Leutnant Horst Anders of 1./KG 2, the bomber coming down in the sea 13 miles south of Dungeness at 2210 hrs on its return flight from London. The time and location of the Do 217's demise matches Hall's claim.

Hauptmann Kurt Seyfarth initially served as a transport pilot prior to joining KG 2 in March 1943. A member of *Stab*./KG 2, he is seen here briefing crews for an attack on London during Operation *Steinbock*. Seyfarth was awarded the *Ritterkreuz* in September 1944, and he survived the war

As a result of these losses, and the onset of bad weather, just one more attack was flown on the night of 29–30 January. A further 12 Ju 88s, two Ju 188s, one He 177 and one Do 217 were destroyed. The latter aircraft, an M-1 flown by Unteroffizier Karl-Heinz Noss of 9./KG 2, was lost without trace during the attack on London.

The first two nights of *Steinbock* had cost I. and III./KG 2 22 aircrew killed and two captured. It was clear that as a result of poor training, inadequate equipment and the superiority of British defences, German bomber units were now being bled dry. Added to this, the withdrawal of about 100 bombers to Italy following the Allied landing at Anzio, codenamed Operation *Shingle*, on 22 January meant the force now available for the offensive was far from adequate. Nevertheless, small-scale raids took place on five nights during the first two weeks of February, followed by more successful attacks using larger-calibre bombs on the nights of the 18th, 20th, 22nd, 23rd and 24th, but with continued heavy losses – indeed, eight Do 217s were lost in attacks on London during the course of the month.

Steinbock then fizzled out, leaving the now-depleted Luftwaffe to prepare for the inevitable Allied invasion over the next three months. During this period, there were few serviceable Do 217s available for I. and III./KG 2.

In the wake of the Allied landings at Anzio and Nettuno, the only Do 217 units remaining in southern France were *Stab* and II./KG 100 at Toulouse. Their first successes off the invasion beaches came on 23 January when the destroyer HMS *Janus* was sunk by an Hs 293 and sister-ship HMS *Jervis* had its bow blown off. Although 80 crew were rescued from *Janus*, at least 161 were killed, including the ship's captain, Lt Cdr William Morrison. The only casualty suffered by II./KG 100 that day was when Hauptmann Hans Eberthäuser of the *Stab* crashed on take-off from Toulouse. The crew survived with injuries.

Over the next four weeks, II./KG 100 would claim a further nine ships sunk off Anzio, including the light cruiser HMS *Spartan* on 29 January, and seven damaged. The *Gruppe*'s last success came on 25 February, when it sank the destroyer HMS *Inglefield* on 25 February. II./KG 100 lost seven Do 217E-5s, resulting in the deaths of 22 experienced aircrew, during the Anzio campaign. The most serious loss came on 16 February when, following an attack the previous day, Hauptmann Heinz-Emil Middermann, *Gruppenkommandeur* of II./KG 100, was returning to Toulouse from Bergamo, in northern Italy, when his bomber suffered an engine failure and crashed at Gambolo, southeast of Novarra, killing him and five others on board the aircraft. Amongst the latter were Oberleutnante Werner Eckert and Dietrich Schreiber, II./KG 100's communications and operations officers, respectively.

By the end of February, the only Do 217E-5 *Staffeln* to remain operational in this theatre were Hauptmann Wolfgang Vorpahl's 5./KG 100 and Hauptmann Willi Scholl's 6./KG 100, as well as *Stab* II./KG 100. Both units subsequently flew their surviving Do 217E-5s alongside Ju 88s from KG 26 and KG 77 in attacks on Allied convoys in the Mediterranean. On 8 March, the target was convoy KMS-43 'Hannah', and the aircraft of Leutnant Kurt Osterwald from 6./KG 100 was shot down by a Beaufighter from No 153 Sqn off Algiers. Although five vessels were claimed as damaged by the German crews, none were sunk.

During the evening of 29 March convoy KMS-45 'Thumbs Up' was targeted by *Stab* II./KG 100 and 5. and 6. *Staffeln*, with a single aircraft from each unit being lost – two fell victim to No 153 Sqn and the third ditched due to engine trouble. Three crewmen were captured and the rest were killed.

The final attack of note came during the evening of 20 April when the convoys UGS-38 'Whoopee' and 'Donaghue II' were targeted. Four vessels were sunk (the troopship *El Biar*, the cargo ship *Royal Star*, the Liberty ship SS *Paul Hamilton* and the destroyer USS *Lansdale* (DD-426)) and two damaged by III./KG 26, I. and III./KG 77 and II./KG 100. The attackers paid a heavy price for this success, however, with four Ju 88s from KG 77, one Ju 88 from III./KG 26, four Ju 88C-6/R-2 fighter escorts from I. and III./ZG 1 and two Do 217E-5s from 6./KG 100 being lost. The Dornier flown by Oberfeldwebel Heinz Kostropetsch ditched at Istres with all four crew wounded, while the aircraft commanded by *Staffelkapitän* Hauptmann Willi Scholl ditched off the Algerian coast. The only claims for Do 217s were again filed by Beaufighter crews of No 153 Sqn, who, in total, claimed one bomber destroyed, one probably destroyed and three damaged.

At the end of April both 5. and 6./KG 100 departed Istres for Toulouse, where they rejoined II./KG 100 as the *Gruppe* tried to convert to the He 177.

Meanwhile, back in northwest Europe, March 1944 would see four major attacks on London, one on Hull on the night of the 19th and then, on 27–28 March, a disastrous raid on Bristol. Both the Hull and Bristol attacks were almost farcical, with bombs being scattered all around the Yorkshire port city and the surrounding counties for the loss of a Ju 188 (flown by the pathfinder leader Hauptmann Walter Schmitt of 2./KG 66), an

He 177, two Do 217M-1s (from 2. and 7./KG 2 to Mosquito nightfighters from Nos 25 and 264 Sqns) and five Ju 88s. Not a single bomb fell on Bristol, despite 112 bombers being plotted mainly over the West Country. Three Ju 188s, nine Ju 88s and a Do 217 (from III./KG 2) were lost, the latter machine being the last of nine Dorniers destroyed in March. British defences were simply erasing Luftwaffe bombers and their crews.

Hardly a sortie was flown for the first two weeks of April, and when they were, losses always occurred. The first major attack, on London, took place on the night of the 18th, and it again saw the loss of a single Do 217M-1 (from 7./KG 2, which was probably damaged by Flg Off Bernard Travers of No 25 Sqn – the aircraft crashed at Schiphol upon its return), eight Ju 88s, four Ju 188s, three Me 410s and an He 177. Sixty bombers targeted Hull again on the night of 20 April, and despite no ordnance falling on the city, four Ju 188s, five Ju 88s, two Do 217M-1s (from 9./KG 2) and an He 177 were shot down. One of the Dorniers fell to an intruder at the very end of the mission just minutes before it landed at Gilze-Rijen.

It was becoming clear to the Allies that in addition to London, English ports were now being targeted in the vain attempt to adversely affect the build-up to the invasion of northwest France. Bristol was the focal point for 70 bombers on 23–24 April, and one Do 217M-1 from 9./KG 2 was amongst the 12 aircraft that failed to return from the mission. Portsmouth saw four ineffective attacks starting on the 25th (two Do 217s from 7./KG 2 were lost in the first of two raids), and then it was Plymouth's turn on the night of the 29th.

The latter mission was an unusual attack in that Do 217Ks of III./KG 100 tried to target the battleship HMS *King George V* using '*Fritz X*'. The *Gruppe* had done very little since moving from Foggia to Toulouse-Blagnac at the start of October 1943. After a few weeks of inactivity, it was then transferred to Eggebek, in northern Germany, for training, prior to moving to Toulouse-Francazal in mid-February 1944 to carry out yet more training. The attack on Plymouth was the unit's first operation for nearly seven months.

A '*Fritz X*' mounted on the fuselage bomb rack of an He 177. Weighing 1400 kg, the unpowered guided weapon was released from an altitude of around 20,000 ft and achieved an impact velocity close to the speed of sound by the time it struck the target. This meant that the '*Fritz X*' could penetrate the deck armour of a heavy cruiser or battleship. On 29 April 1944, III./KG 100 planned on using the weapon against warships moored in Plymouth Sound

The intended target on 29 April 1944 was the battleship HMS *King George V*. A combination of poor weather, anti-aircraft fire and fighters meant the attack was a failure. Two crews were lost, including that of Hauptmann Herbert Pfeffer, *Gruppenkommandeur* of III./KG 100

In darkness on the morning of 29 April, 15 aircraft from 8. and 9./KG 100, each carrying a single *'Fritz X'*, took off from Toulouse-Francazal for Orléans. At the latter airfield, crews met with their *Gruppenkommandeur*, Hauptmann Herbert Pfeffer, who had been visiting Garz/Usedorm (the base for *Lehr-und Erprobungskommando* 36, the unit responsible for developing the Hs 293 and *'Fritz X'*) following a meeting in Berlin. That afternoon, the crews were briefed on their target and the tactics to be employed. None had any experience of dropping *'Fritz X'* at night, and for many crews, including Hauptmann Pfeffer's, this would be their first operational mission with the bomb.

It is believed that only 12 aircraft took off from Orléans on the night of the 29th and headed to Morlaix, in Brittany, where they would pick up the Knickebein blind bombing beam and follow it to Plymouth. They would then use the same beam to head for Toulouse after the attack. The target was meant to be illuminated by Ju 188s from I./KG 66, but it would appear they were either late, or the Do 217s early, as when the first aircraft arrived over Plymouth at 0330 hrs on the 30th, no flares were seen. Furthermore, a mist and a smoke screen further obscured the port.

Minimal damage was subsequently inflicted on Plymouth, let alone the warship, and two Ju 88s and two Fw 190s were lost. In addition, two Do 217s were also destroyed. The K-3 flown by Leutnant Herbert Palme of 9./KG 100 was the fourth aircraft to take off from Orléans, and as he approached Plymouth, his ailerons jammed. He then made a guess at where his target was and dropped the *'Fritz X'*. Minutes later, the bomber was illuminated by searchlights, blinding Palme. He quickly lost control of the aircraft, which fell into a spin and crashed near Totnes.

The second K-3 destroyed was the aircraft flown by the *Gruppenkommandeur*, Hauptmann Pfeffer. Upon reaching the target area, the crew could see nothing, forcing them to orbit four times. The bomber was soon illuminated by searchlights, the pilot blinded and the starboard engine set on fire. The bomb was jettisoned and the crew attempted to bail out, but Pfeffer and his observer, Feldwebel Heinrich Penz, were killed when the bomber crashed south of Plymouth. The two survivors managed to swim ashore, and later told their interrogators the bomber had either been shot down by ground fire or that the pilot had lost control. However,

Sqn Ldr David Williams of Mosquito-equipped No 406 Sqn was credited with two Do 217s, noting in his combat report;

'A free chase to a well illuminated target due south was then made and AI contact was obtained at five-mile range on a violently jinking target which was identified as a Do 217, and attack was made at minimum range while the enemy aircraft was still illuminated. Hits were seen on the starboard engine causing immediate flames to spread and pieces were seen to fall off the wing. The aircraft then spun straight in, landing on ground and control reported a body found.

'A second contact had been held at two miles range to starboard, which was then followed out to sea, jinking violently. This was also identified as a Do 217 and attack was made at 100 yards with a short burst on the starboard side; the enemy bursting into flames, turning on its back and crashing into the sea.'

Sqn Ldr Williams was destined to engage III./KG 100 again, this time in daylight, in just under three months' time.

Away from the Mediterranean and northwest Europe, Do 217 operations were very few and far between. The J-model nightfighter had by now been all but replaced by the Do 217N, with surviving examples of the former being used by the training unit NJG 101. Even then, there were far fewer Do 217 nightfighters in frontline service than there were Bf 110s and Ju 88s. Nevertheless, NJG 4, NJG 100 and 4./NJG 200 continued to use the Do 217N in ever decreasing numbers. 4./NJG 200 eventually stopped flying the N-model in May 1944, with NJG 4 following suit in June and NJG 100 in October.

The *Nachtaufklärungsstaffeln* also continued to fly the Do 217, but again in ever dwindling numbers. For example, 3. *Nachtaufklärungsstaffel* was taken off operations in May 1944 pending being re-equipped with a reconnaissance version of the Arado Ar 234 jet bomber, after which it would be re-designated 1.(F)/123.

A handful of Do 217s were also in use with secondary test and evaluation units through to war's end, with a K-3 from *Lehr-und Erprobungskommando* 36 being reportedly shot down by fighters near Öttingen. Pilot Oberleutnant Harald Englisch and crewman Stabsfeldwebel Hermann Grothaus were both killed. Mustang pilot 1Lt William C Reese of the 364th Fighter Squadron (FS)/357th Fighter Group (FG) reported shooting down a Do 217 near Augsburg at 1155 hrs that day, Öttingen being 65 km south of that location.

On the Channel Front, it was now a matter of hurry up and wait for the inevitable invasion, with the Luftwaffe proving increasingly impotent in its attempts to delay preparations for the Normandy landings. Bristol was

Sqn Ldr David Williams of No 406 Sqn accounted for both the Do 217s lost by III./KG 100 during the attack on *King George V*. He would down a third bomber from the *Gruppe* on 21 July 1944

Many older aircraft were assigned to secondary roles, including this Do 217K-1 which served as an executive transport with *Flugbereitschaft Luftflotte* 2. The insignia of the latter organisation, applied to the fuselage immediately aft of the cockpit glazing, consisted of a blue shield, a silver eagle, yellow, crossed, Feldmarschall's batons and the number '2'. This unit, which flew a mix of Do 217E-4s and K-1s in 1943, recorded its first loss (Wk-Nr 4481 F5+LH) on 20 February and its last (Wk-Nr 4611 F5+LK) on 31 December. Note that this aircraft also has a white Mediterranean fuselage band

attacked on the night of 14–15 May, followed by Portsmouth 24 hours later, with the inevitable result in respect to losses – five Ju 88s, seven Ju 188s and four Do 217s (all from 7./KG 2) were lost over the two nights. 7. *Staffel* had 13 aircrew killed and three captured, with all the Dorniers falling to nightfighters.

Operation *Overlord* on 6 June 1944 signalled the beginning of the end for the Do 217 as a conventional bomber. Due to Allied air superiority over much of France and the Low Countries, KG 2 had been operating from airfields well inside Germany since January 1944. So, to reach Normandy, crews had to either forward base at those French or Dutch airfields deemed safe enough from Allied air attacks, or face longer trips from Germany and run the risk of meeting enemy intruders.

Bombing and mining missions began on the evening of 6 June, with two waves being flown on a number of nights. By the start of June 1944 only III./KG 2 was still equipped with the Do 217, and the *Gruppe*'s attacks were rarely made by more than nine aircraft. On 22 June, III./KG 2 handed its aircraft over to I./KG 2 and moved to Friedrichshafen, where it was hoped pilots would convert to the Do 335 – something that never happened. Instead, crews switched to the Ju 88 and formed V./NJG 2, commanded by Major Albert Schreiweis. From now on, I./KG 2 – operating with no more than 16 aircraft – was the only *Gruppe* within the *Geschwader* still flying operationally.

Combat losses were relatively light due to the reduced number of Do 217s in service, with 11 bombers being lost to all causes in both June and July. August 1944 would be I./KG 2's final month of operations, and at least 12 aircraft were lost in action or accidents, with additional examples being destroyed in bombing or strafing attacks on airfields in Germany. Among the Dorniers shot down was the final Do 217 to crash on

British soil. On the night of 22–23 August, the M-1 of Feldwebel Lukas Jooss from 3./KG 2 was shot down by anti-aircraft artillery at Dover while flying in solid cloud. The bomber crashed near Elham, in Kent, killing the crew. Quite what this aircraft was doing over England is not clear as no bombs were either dropped from the Dornier or found in the wreckage.

It would appear that the last Do 217 bombers to be shot down in combat fell on 5 September when three Dorniers were reportedly attacked by USAAF fighters. Capt Gordon S Burlingame of the Thunderbolt-352nd FS/353rd FG reported shooting one of the aircraft down near Apeldoorn, in the Netherlands, at 1130 hrs.

Do 217E-1 Wk-Nr 5094 served with pilot training unit *Flugzeugführerschule* (C) 5 until it was destroyed in an accident at Usadel, near Lake Tollensee in Germany, on 7 February 1944. Student pilot Leutnant Harald von Laak and engineer Unteroffizier Walter Börner were both killed in the crash

KG 2 was disbanded on 3 October. Most pilots went to single-seat fighter units and the remaining aircrew were dispersed throughout the Luftwaffe, most being used in ground roles.

That left III./KG 100 as the only bomber unit still struggling on with Do 217, the *Gruppe* receiving examples of the M-11 powered by DB 603A-2 engines driving four-bladed propellers. The aircraft's bomb-bay had been redesigned to accommodate the tail unit of the '*Fritz X*', while its defensive armament now consisted of three MG 131s, two MG 81s and a *Rüstsatz 23* (R23) modification comprising a pair of rear-firing MG 81Zs in the tail. 6./KG 100 was the first *Staffel* to be re-equipped with the M-11, after which it exchanged places with 8./KG 100.

Following the Normandy invasion, III./KG 100 had soon found itself in action over the beaches targeting Allied shipping just offshore. On 8 June, the unit was credited with damaging the Landing Ship Headquarters HMS *Buolo* and sinking the destroyer HMS *Lawford*, with 37 crew being killed when the latter went down. However, these successes came at a cost, with *Stab* III./KG 100 losing a K-3 and 6./KG 100 an E-5. Both were shot down into the Baie de Seine by anti-aircraft fire, with the crews of Oberleutnant Oskar Schmidtke and Oberfeldwebel Bruno Obst being killed.

Two nights later, 6. *Staffel* lost its first two M-11s, while 9. *Staffel* had a K-3 destroyed. Again, all three bombers fell to anti-aircraft fire, two crashing on land on the way back to base and the third coming down in the Baie de Seine. There were no survivors. 13 June would see the sinking of the destroyer HMS *Boadicea* 16 miles southwest of Portland, with only 12 of its crew of 182 being rescued. It was thought at the time that the vessel had been hit by an Hs 293, but it is now believed the destroyer was sunk by a torpedo dropped by a Ju 88 from KG 77. On 15 June, a Do 217K-3 of 7./KG 100 fell to anti-aircraft fire off Cherbourg, and two aircraft from 9./KG 100 (a K-2 and a K-3) crashed on their return flight to base. There were no survivors from all three aircraft. Just one more aircraft was destroyed in June – a Do 217K-3 of 7./KG 100 was lost over the beachhead on the 25th, killing Leutnant Roland Faude and his crew.

On the night of 4 July, in a 'major' attack by eight Do 217s from III./KG 100 and three He 177s of I./KG 40 against shipping in the Orne Estuary, *Stab* III./KG 100 lost a K-3, 7. *Staffel* a K-3 and two M-11s and 8. and 9. *Staffel* a K-3 each. Nightfighter pilots Sqn Ldr Bill Gill of No 125 Sqn and Plt Off Stan Williams of No 456 Sqn claimed one Do 217 destroyed apiece, while American Flt Off Richard Seage flying a Mosquito with No 21 Sqn was credited with damaging a Dornier in the Loire area. It is possible that Seage's claim was an aircraft from 9. *Staffel*, flown by Leutnant Ludwig Schäfer, which was reported lost over the Gironde Estuary. Of the 22 crew shot down, only Leutnant Erich Keller (*Gruppe* Technical Officer), Obergefreiter Hans Menne of 7. *Staffel* and Leutnant Siegfried Kynast of 8. *Staffel* survived the experience to be captured.

Further missions continued throughout July, with losses on the 17th and 20th. On 21 July, there was a change from night to day operations, with the usual consequences ensuing for the beleaguered Do 217 crews. That morning, a cruiser and at least two destroyers of the 14th Destroyer Escort Group were sighted off Brest, so six aircraft, each loaded with Hs 293s, took off from Toulouse-Blagnac at 1045 hrs. They flew to the Bay of Biscay and then headed north along the coast in pairs. At 1320 hrs, when southwest of Ushant, crews spotted not only their targets but two Mosquitos of No 406 Sqn (led by Sqn Ldr David Williams), two Mosquitos of No 235 Sqn (led by Wg Cdr John Yonge) and two Mosquitos of No 248 Sqns (led by Flt Lt Fred Passey). The result was inevitable, as Sqn Ldr Williams recalled;

'The weather in England was solid fog, and Group asked for volunteers to defend some Navy destroyers. We took off following the runway lights and proceeded to the rendezvous. On approaching the ships, I spotted two Do 217s making a run from the southwest. I closed on the nearest one and opened fire. I observed hits, and the aircraft either ditched or crashed into the sea. I had been caught in a crossfire and my starboard engine was shot out. I feathered it and started to attack the remaining Dornier. In spite of two cannons being jammed, I opened fire and observed hits. Before I could

This Do 217M-1, coded K7+AH, of 1./*Nachtaufklärungsstaffel* was captured at Linz-Hörsching, in Austria. Note the spirals on the spinners

finish the kill, the crew members started bailing out. As the aircraft was not heading in the direction of the destroyers, I pulled back and informed the Navy there were aircrew in the ocean. Before I could close to finish the kill, a Coastal Command Mosquito closed in and shot it down. I believe they credited me with a shared kill.'

Wg Cdr Yonge reported that at 1320 hrs they spotted two Do 217s in echelon to port, which they immediately attacked, one exploding in the air the other crashing into the sea. Flt Lt Passey noted in his combat report;

'Sighted unidentified aircraft crash in the sea and explode and the survivors picked up by a surface vessel. At 1337 hrs, a Do 217 was sighted and both aircraft attacked, and claim to have destroyed the enemy aircraft. At 1348 hrs a second Do 217 was sighted and engaged, scoring numerous strikes. The enemy aircraft dived into cloud and is probably destroyed.'

The first two Dorniers lost were the aircraft of Oberleutnant Karl Lamp, the *Staffelführer* of 9./KG 100, who was leading the unit while Oberleutnant Helmut Dietrich recovered from wounds received in an air attack on Toulouse-Blagnac on 23 June, and the Do 217 flown by Unteroffizier Gustav Schmidt and a scratch crew from 7., 8. and 9./KG 100. All bar one of Lamp's crew survived the ordeal, and Schmidt's crew were captured. Amongst the latter was Unteroffizier Georg Dabitz, who recalled post-war;

'After our night mission on 20 July from Blagnac airfield near Toulouse, Unteroffizier Peters was unable to attend the flight briefing on 21 July at 0800 hrs due to having sinusitis. Despite our protest, Unteroffizier Hopfgartner and I were assigned to Unteroffizier Gustav Schmidt of 7. *Staffel*, who was completely unknown to me, as was Beobachter Unteroffizier August Reidenbach from 8. *Staffel*.

'Six Do 217s equipped with Hs 293 guided missiles were to take off at 1000 hrs. Departure time was delayed by hours because the promised fighter escort from JG 51 in Lyon failed to materialise. There was a nervousness at the air base triggered by the assassination attempt on Hitler on 20 July. Finally, around noon, take-off was ordered.

Do 217J-1 G3+PV of II./NJG 101, this *Gruppe* being one of the last nightfighter units to operate both the J-1 and N-1. Note the radar aerials have been removed from this aircraft, which has been adorned with the 'England Blitz' insignia adopted by a number of Luftwaffe nightfighter units

This seemingly intact Do 217M-1 was found at Prague Ruzyně airfield, in then Czechoslovakia, post-war. The fuselage code K7+EK suggests that the aircraft had been assigned to 2./*Nachtaufklärungsstaffel* in the final months of the conflict in Europe

'We flew next to Oberleutnant Lamp. There was no trace of a fighter escort. To the left of us, approximately 60 km away, were two more aircraft heading north, with the remaining two 60 km to the right of us near the coast. I did not know the names of these crews. Suddenly, the radio operator, who was sitting behind us in the swivel chair at the machine gun, reported, "Enemy fighters in sight!", and very soon our aeroplane was hit. We were lucky that, at this point, we were flying at zero altitude above the water.

'The emergency ditching took place with the two Hs 293 guided missiles still under the wings. The "colossus" glided on the water for a few seconds. Now everything had to happen quickly to climb out of the sinking coffin. My life was literally hanging by a thread. The emergency exit hatch jammed due to the impact. I pulled the hatch lever with desperation. The water was almost up to my neck. Somehow, I managed to open the exit. How I was able free myself from this situation is a mystery to me. I probably owe my survival to my Kapok life jacket, as it gave me buoyancy to get through an opening above my head. So I got outside, where there was not much left to see of the aeroplane.

'I urgently needed to get away from the sinking Do 217 so as not to be pulled down by it. Then a new fight began. Somehow, the handle of my back-pack parachute had got stuck and opened the parachute packaging bag. Rigging lines and the parachute loosened and wrapped around my body and legs. Now I was fighting the waves and the ballast of the parachute, which I could not get rid of.

'My comrades were already in their rubber dinghies. They were about 200 m from me. When they recognised my difficult situation, they came to my aid. Now, I was able to inflate my one-man inflatable boat. Thank God, the boat was still intact, and I soon sat in it. While the Mosquitos kept flying over us, we bound our boats together and waited for our fate. After two hours we recognised the outline of an English destroyer in the distance. It came closer, and soon we were prisoners of war.'

The final aircraft lost was flown by Leutnant Wolfgang Schirmer of 8./KG 100 – none of its crew survived. In addition to the damage to Sqn

Ldr Williams' Mosquito, the other No 406 Sqn aircraft flown by Flg Off Bill Meakin was damaged by debris from a stricken Do 217 and Flt Sgt Walter Scott of No 248 Sqn failed to return.

August would see continued attacks against shipping off the Normandy coast, as well as raids on the strategically important Pontaubault and Pontorson bridges. The first of these took place on the night of the 3rd when six Do 217s from III./KG 100 targeted the bridges with glide-bombs in the first such standoff missile attack on a land target. The bridge raids would cost the *Gruppe* nine more bombers.

Then, following Operation *Dragoon* (the Allied invasion of Provence, in southern France) on 15 August, III./KG 100 was sent to attack shipping off Saint-Raphaël. The *Gruppe* claimed to have damaged or sunk three landing craft and a destroyer, although these claims are not fully corroborated by Allied records – an Hs 293 certainly sank LST-282 on 15 August, however. Three aircraft were lost to the ships' defensive fire, with the Do 217M-1 flown by Oberfeldwebel Rudolf Freiberg of 7./KG 100 crashing off Pamplona, in Spain. The crew was rescued by Spanish fishermen, and together with the crew of Feldwebel Helmut Germann's Do 217K-3 from 9. *Staffel*, all were interned. Finally, the M-11 of 8./KG 100 flown by Oberfeldwebel Rudolf Blab disappeared without trace.

Two days later, III./KG 100 was ordered to transfer to Germany, and on 18 and 19 August it withdrew to Garz and was disbanded. Groundcrew who could not be flown out had to return by road, and they were constantly attacked by the Maquis – they suffered more than 300 casualties. KG 100's final loss came on 19 August when the Do 217 flown by Feldwebel Wilhelm Krag was shot down over Auzon, in south-central France, on its way to Germany by F6F Hellcats of Ens Charles Hullard and Lt Edwin Castanedo of VF-74 flying from the escort carrier USS *Kasaan Bay* (CVE-69) sailing off the French Riviera.

It is believed that some of the aircraft and crews formerly assigned to KG 100 were retained by *Lehr-und Erprobungskommando* 36, which was renamed *Versuchskommando*/KG 200 at the end of 1944. On 10 March 1945 the unit reported it had nine Do 217s available to support attacks on bridges planned for the 13th, but the full details of what occurred on

These propless Do 217M-1s were three of six from 2./Nachtaufklärungsstaffel captured at the end of the war at Beldringe, near Odense in Denmark. The unit had moved to this airfield on 1 May 1945. It has been stated that the middle aircraft was Wk-Nr 56527 U5+HK – indeed, the letters +HK are visible on the fuselage in this photograph. It was subsequently flown to the RAE at Farnborough and put on display there in October–November 1945, having been given the code AIR MIN 106

that date are not known. It is believed the Do 217s of *Versuchskommando/* KG 200 flew their last mission on 12 April when crews attempted to down bridges over the River Oder with Hs 293s.

For the remaining eight months of the war, the only units that appear to have been using the Do 217 in an operational role were II./NJG 101, whose last combat loss was on 18 September 1944 when Leutnant Hans-Joachim Beck collided with a Soviet Il-4 bomber over the Mátra mountain range, 130 km east of Budapest, and 1., 2. and 4. *Nachtaufklärungsstaffel*. Precise details pertaining to the operations flown by the nightfighter *Gruppe* and the reconnaissance *Staffeln* on the Eastern Front are scant.

POSTSCRIPT

The production of the Do 217 finished in October 1943, at which point further development of the aircraft ceased. It had been intended to have M-2 (torpedo), M-3 (dive-bomber), M-4 and M-8 (both high-altitude bombers) and M-9 and M-10 (both guided-missile carriers) variants, but these projects either failed to make it off the drawing board or were cancelled. The only variant that just about made it into frontline service was the Do 217M-11, which was designed specifically for the *'Fritz X'* and Hs 293 missiles. Just 40 M-11s were built, and they were used operationally in very limited numbers by KG 100 over the Normandy beaches and in opposition to the invasion of Southern France between June and August 1944. As usual with many late-war German aircraft, they arrived too late and in too small a number to make any difference.

Following VE Day, the remains of Do 217s were found scattered over numerous airfields in Europe. Yet despite a number being captured intact, no examples of what legendary Fleet Air Arm test pilot Capt Eric 'Winkle' Brown called 'the pregnant pencil' exist. 'Writing an epitaph for this last of the Dornier bomber line to see combat', Brown noted in 1975, 'one would perhaps say that it had been a moderate aircraft which established an undistinguished but honourable operational record.'

Do 217M-1 Wk-Nr 56158 was amongst the Dorniers from 2./*Nachtaufklärungsstaffel* captured at Beldringe. It too was flown to Farnborough, where the bomber had the code AIR MIN 107 applied as seen here. Also displayed by the RAE, Wk-Nr 56158 had been placed in storage at Brize Norton, in Oxfordshire, by December 1945. It was then moved to Sealand, in North Wales, before finally being scrapped at Bicester, also in Oxfordshire, in 1956

APPENDICES

Do 217 BOMBER AND RECONNAISSANCE COMBAT UNITS

I., II. and III./KG 2

II./KG 40

IV./KG 3

II. and III./KG 100

I. and II./KG 101

Lehr-und Erprobungskommando 17 (becomes 15./KG 6 9/42 and I./KG 66 4/43)

Kampfgruppe zur besonderen Verwendung 21 (becomes *Lehr-und Erprobungskommando* 21 then III./KG 100 4/43)

Lehr-und Erprobungskommando 36 (becomes *Versuchskommando*/KG 200 12/44-1/45)

Versuchsstaffel 293 (becomes *Lehr-und Erprobungskommando* 15 and then forms II./KG 100 5/43)

1. *Nachtaufklärungsstaffel*

2. *Nachtaufklärungsstaffel*

3. *Nachtaufklärungsstaffel* (to 5/44)

4. *Nachtaufklärungsstaffel*

4. (*Nacht*)/ *Fernaufklärungsgruppe*

Horch-und Störstaffel 2 and 4./*Fernaufklärungsgruppe* 5

6.(F)/*Aufklärungsgruppe* 123

II./*Fernaufklärungsgeschwader* 101

Do 217 NIGHTFIGHTER UNITS

II./NJG 1

Ergänzungsstaffel, I., II. and III./NJG 2

I., II., III. and VI./NJG 3

I., II. and III./NJG 4

II. and 12./NJG 5

I. and II./NJG 100

I., II. and 7./NJG 101

4./NJG 200

Nachtjagdschule 1

Führer Kurier Staffel

Nachtjagdkommando Oberbefehlshaber Süd

235ª *Squadriglia*, 60° *Gruppo*, 41° *Stormo Intercettori*

COLOUR PLATES

1
Do 217 V4 Wk-Nr 690 D-AMSD of the *Erprobungsstelle der Luftwaffe*, Rechlin, Germany, June 1939

The fourth Do 217 prototype first flew in May 1939, and it was used to evaluate the aircraft's performance when fitted with the Jumo 211A or B engines. Various bomb loads were also trialled with this aircraft while it was at the *Erprobungsstelle der Luftwaffe* in 1939, and the following year the V4 undertook wind-assisted catapult take-off tests, after which it was returned to the Dornier factory at Friedrichshafen-Löwental in February 1941. Wk-Nr 690 was subsequently used for the development of quick-release engines and, upon returning to Rechlin, participated in braking parachute trials – by then it had been allotted the code CN+HL.

2
Do 217A-0 T5+MH of 1./*Aufklärungsgruppe Oberbefehlshaber der Luftwaffe*, Berlin Werder, Germany, February 1940

Just six Do 217A-0s (Wk-Nr 2701 to 2706) were produced, these aircraft being fitted with two Rb 50/30 cameras in the cockpit and an Rb 20/30 camera in the fuselage. Powered initially by DB 601A or B engines, these aircraft were assigned to 1./*Aufklärungsgruppe Oberbefehlshaber der Luftwaffe* at the start of January 1940 but their time in service with this unit was short. Later flown by units such as 10./KG 2 and IV./KG 40 as aircrew trainers, the last recorded mention of a Do 217A-0 was on 30 March 1942 when Wk-Nr 2703, flying with 10./KG 2, was apparently lost in an accident near Osnabrück.

3
Do 217E-1 Wk-Nr 5069 U5+DN of 5./KG 2, Evreux, France, October 1941

This aircraft, flown by Oberleutnant Günther Dolenga, took off from Evreux at 0100 hrs on 12 October 1941 on a shipping reconnaissance west of the Isles of Scilly. Due to strong winds and false bearings transmitted by the RAF, the crew became totally lost, and thinking they were over France, force-landed at Jury's Gap Sewer, in Broomhill near Rye, East Sussex, at 0505 hrs. They were all quickly captured by local troops. Being a Do 217E-1, it did not have a turret at the rear of the cockpit. Nevertheless, it was armed with a forward-firing MG 151 and three rear-firing MG 15s. Bearing two ship silhouettes (for vessels sunk or damaged) on its port fin, Wk-Nr 5069 was the first Do 217 to be captured almost intact.

4
Do 217E-2 Wk-Nr 1145 U5+ZN of 5./KG 2, Soesterberg, the Netherlands, March 1942

This aircraft has not been camouflaged for night operations, which would probably indicate it has recently been delivered to Hauptmann Heinz Engel's 5./KG 2. The bomber, which was subsequently upgraded to E-4 standard, suffered considerable damage after a tyre burst while landing at Vannes on 11 August 1943. Unteroffizier Ulrich Bachmann and his crew were uninjured in the accident, and there is no mention made of the aircraft after this date.

5
Do 217E-4 Wk-Nr 4279 F8+CN of 5./KG 40, Soesterberg, the Netherlands, July 1942

This aircraft was widely photographed prior to being shot down during a night attack on an airframe factory in Bedford on 23 July 1942. Note the clear demarcation between the upper- and undersurface camouflage, which appears to have been peculiar to Do 217s assigned to II./KG 40. Note also the clear code on the tail in white, while the fuselage code was all but painted over. Flown by Oberleutnant Heinrich Viess, this aircraft was jointly shot down by No 486 Sqn's Flt Lt Harvey Sweetman, who was flying a Hurricane, and Flt Lt Ted McMillan of Beaufighter-equipped No 409 Sqn. The crew, however, who all bailed out and were captured, credited their demise to a single-seat fighter.

6
Do 217E-4 Wk-Nr 5502 F8+AP of 3./KG 2, Gilze-Rijen, the Netherlands, September 1942

The reason why a crew from 3./KG 2 was lost flying in a Do 217 from 6./KG 40 is initially not clear. On 22 April 1942, Wk-Nr 5368 became the first of four Do 217s coded F8+AP of 6./KG 40 to be destroyed that year when it was written off in an accident. Then, on 2 August, this aircraft, recorded as with 3./KG 2, suffered minor combat damage. The bomber was destroyed on 8 September when it was shot down by Flg Off Alex McRitchie of No 151 Sqn over Orwell, in Cambridgeshire, killing Feldwebel Alfred Witting and his crew. On 2 October, Wk-Nr 5582 F8+AP of 6./KG 40 was lost in an accident, and, finally, on 18 December, Wk-Nr 4384 F8+AP was shot down south of Shoreham, in West Sussex. It is, therefore, assumed that II./KG 40 loaned Wk-Nr 5502 to KG 2 for a short period following the losses the latter *Geschwader* had suffered during the summer and, specifically, over Dieppe on 19 August 1942.

7
Do 217E-4 Wk-Nr 4272 U5+NT of 9./KG 2, Deelen, the Netherlands, October 1942

This aircraft has been fitted with tail-mounted fixed twin MG 81Z machine guns – the so-called R23 field modification. This required a crewman to use a periscope fitted in the cockpit to see backwards. The bomber is in standard night camouflage and has the Werknummer and last two letters of the code on the tail. It would be lost attacking Lincoln on the night on 15–16 January 1943, by which time the aircraft had been re-coded U5+AT. Flown by Unteroffizier Hans Unglaube on its final mission, the bomber was probably shot down into the North Sea by Flt Lt Joe Singleton of No 25 Sqn, resulting in the deaths of the four crew.

8
Do 217E-4 Wk-Nr 4377 U5+FL of 3./KG 2, Cognac, France, November 1942

In response to the Allied *Torch* landings in Morocco, Algeria and Tunisia in the hours before daybreak on 8 November 1942, *Stab*, I., II. and IV./KG 2 moved to Cognac, in western France. Aircraft were painted with the white Mediterranean fuselage bands and, additionally, had white bands applied around the wings outboard of the engines and the undersides of the cowlings painted yellow.

On 15 November 1942, II./KG 2 returned to Eindhoven. This aircraft, flown by Unteroffizier Konrad Schelke, would be lost mine-laying off Dover on the night of 8 February 1943 – all four crew were killed.

9
Do 217E-4 Wk-Nr 5562 U5+LS of 8./KG 2, Deelen, the Netherlands, November 1942

This bomber still wears the markings given to aircraft countering the Allied landings in North Africa in November 1942. Following its return to Deelen, these markings were eventually removed. Wk-Nr 5562 suffered engine failure shortly after taking off to attack Hull on 9 March 1943, and it was totally destroyed during a forced landing at Katwoude, northeast of Amsterdam, at 1940 hrs – just 17 minutes after take-off. Feldwebel Wilhelm Haase and his crew were all injured.

10
Do 217E-4 U5+KS of 8./KG 2, Deelen, the Netherlands, November 1942

This is another aircraft from Hauptmann Walter Scheiner's 8./KG 2 that was rushed to Cognac in Operation *Stockdorf* in November 1942. The lack of any visible Werknummer makes it hard to positively identify this aircraft, but it was probably a replacement for U5+KS Wk-Nr 5446, which crashed at Erches, near Montdidier on 25 May 1942, killing the then *Staffelkapitän* Hauptmann Hubertus Piper, pilot Oberfeldwebel Otto Zöke, two crew and two groundcrew. The next mention of an aircraft bearing the U5+KS code is on 24 March 1944, when Do 217M-1 Wk-Nr 326254 suffered damage in an accident.

11
Do 217E-4 Wk-Nr 5441 U5+BL of 3./KG 2, Gilze-Rijen, the Netherlands, December 1942

This aircraft wears the pale all-over grey low-visibility scheme applied to a small number of Do 217s involved in 'Pirate' pin-point daylight attacks by single aircraft on targets in Britain in 1942–43. With only the BL code in white on the fin and a single B in yellow under the nose (not visible from this angle), the bomber was routinely flown by Oberleutnant Ernst Schneiderbauer of 3./KG 2. He had previously flown Fw 200s with I./KG 40 before transferring to 3./KG 2. Schneiderbauer's usual crew was Unteroffizier Hans Weber (Bordfunker), Oberfeldwebel Gregor Eilbrecht (Bordmechaniker) and Oberfeldwebel Wilhelm Zacharias (Beobachter). However, when Do 217E-4 Wk-Nr 4397 U5+LL suffered an engine failure in an attack on Portsmouth on the night of 7 February 1943, Schneiderbauer was force to crash-land 12 km south-southwest of Gilze-Rijen and Zacharias was injured. New Beobachter Unteroffizier Martin Hoffmann joined the Schneiderbauer crew, and they were duly shot down by a No 219 Sqn Beaufighter in Wk-Nr 5441 while targeting Newcastle on the night of 11 March 1943. All four airmen bailed out (two of them having suffered wounds) and were captured.

12
Do 217J-1 Wk-Nr 1251 GE+EA of 4./NJG 3, Löwental, Germany, December 1942

The first J-1 to be recorded lost was Wk-Nr 1263 of *Ergänzungsstaffel* of NJG 2, which collided with another Do 217 on 28 May 1942. It is possible that the aircraft depicted in this profile was assigned to 4./NJG 3 at around the same time, Wk-Nr 1251 being badly damaged at Westerland-Sylt on 9 July 1942 – the early J-1s came from the 12** and 13** series of Werknummers. Once repaired, Wk-Nr 1251 served with I./NJG 4 until it was damaged in another accident on 22 January 1943. Once returned to airworthiness, the aircraft was flown by II./NJG 101 until it was finally written off in a third accident on 26 March 1944.

13
Do 217E-4 Wk-Nr 4243 U5+GR of 7./KG 2, Deelen, the Netherlands, December 1942

Oberleutnant Rolf Häusner was at the controls of this aircraft when it flew into a hillside at Hawnby, in Yorkshire, at 2240 hrs on 17 December 1942. The Do 217 disintegrated, killing him and his crew instantly. The bodies of Oberfeldwebeln Hartwig Hupe and Ernst Weiderer were recovered and buried, but all that was found of Häusner and his observer, Unteroffizier Syrius Erd, were the shoulder boards of a Hauptmann and an Unteroffizier – it appears that Rolf Häusner had been promoted shortly before his death. Having initially flown Do 17s with 7./KG 2, Häusner had commenced his conversion to the Do 217 at Achmer in July 1941. It would appear that his first operational flight with the aircraft came on 13 January 1942 in U5+BR. In July 1942, Häusner moved to *Stab* III./KG 2, before transferring back to take command of 7./KG 2 in late August 1942 following the capture of Oberleutnant Rudolf Graf von Thun-Hohenstein on the 8th of that month. Häusner would be awarded the *Ehrenpokal* on 16 November 1942.

14
Do 217K-06 Wk-Nr 4406 RD+JE of *Kampfgruppe zur besonderen Verwendung* 21, Schwäbisch Hall, Germany, January 1943

Wk-Nr 4406 was one of the prototype K-model Do 217s, the aircraft being used for aerial torpedo trials at Gotenhafen in early January 1943. On the 21st of that same month, it suffered an accident at Schwäbisch Hall – documentation relating to the incident recorded the bomber as being a Do 217K-1. In March 1943, *Kampfgruppe zur besonderen Verwendung* 21 became part of *Lehr-und Erprobungskommando* 21, which had been formed in September 1942 under the leadership of Hauptmann Ernst Hetzel to undertake trials with the *'Fritz X'*. At the end of April 1943, this unit became III./KG 100, with Hetzel as its *Gruppenkommandeur*.

15
Do 217E-4 F8+BC of *Stab* II./KG 40, Soesterberg, the Netherlands, March 1943

Camouflaged in 'Pirate' attack pale grey overall, this aircraft was the favoured mount of veteran pilot Hauptmann Wilhelm Schmitter in early 1943. Its tail fin is adorned with two victory bars (from 15 August 1940 and 1 July 1941), two factory attack silhouettes (believed to be Leamington Spa on 13 June and 16 July 1942) and three barrage balloons destroyed markings – all claimed by Schmitter, but not all in this Do 217. An experienced maritime pilot prior to switching to bombers, he had flown He 60 floatplanes pre-war and, at the end of April 1940, joined He 115-equipped 1./*Küstenfliegergruppe* 906. Commissioned as a Leutnant in November 1940, Schmitter joined 4./KG 40, flying He 111s, in February 1941. On 1 July that same year, he was credited with shooting down a Hudson of No 206 Sqn. Later that month he converted to the Do 217. Promoted to Oberleutnant in November 1941, Schmitter was awarded the *Deutsches Kreuz* in Gold on 18 May 1942 for completing 143 missions. This was followed by the *Ritterkreuz* on 19 September 1942 after having flown 172 missions. On 1 March 1943, Schmitter was promoted to Hauptmann, and three months later given command of 5./KG 40. Later that month, II./KG 40 converted to the Me 410 and became V./KG 2. He was killed in action on the night of 8 November 1943, and would be posthumously awarded the *Eichenlaub* in March 1944.

16
Do 217M-1 Wk-Nr 56126 Z6+AK of 2./KG 66, Montdidier, France, summer 1943

I./KG 66 received its first M-1s in July 1943, and had a maximum establishment of just eight E-4s, K-1s and M-1s until December 1943. As usual with this unit, its Do 217s had distinctive camouflage and markings. The first M-1 from the *Gruppe* to be lost was Wk-Nr 56019 in an air attack on Montdidier on 24 October 1943, and a second example was destroyed in an accident the following month. After service with I./KG 66, Wk-Nr 56126 was passed on to 3./KG 2, and the aircraft was still serving with the *Staffel* when it crashed near Dorking, in Surrey, at 2156 hrs on 24 February 1944 following the failure of its tail unit. By that time it was carrying the code U5+EL. RAF intelligence noted that the aircraft had a large number 3 painted on the tail, and its *Stammkennzeichen* (factory code) was CL+UA. The bomber's camouflage was described as dull blue with black wavy lines on the uppersurfaces and fuselage sides, while the underside and much of the fin and rudder were black.

17
Do 217J-1 235-4 of 235ª *Squadriglia*, 60° *Gruppo*, 41° *Stormo Intercettori*, Lonate Pozzolo, Italy, July 1943

In August 1942, crews from the Regia Aeronautica began training on the Do 217J-1 in Germany. A total of 12 nightfighters were delivered (six J-1s and six J-2s) to 235ª *Squadriglia*, 60° *Gruppo*, 41° *Stormo Intercettori* at Lonate Pozzolo. 235ª *Squadriglia* was commanded by Capitano Aramis Ammanato, and he recorded the unit's only victory with the Do 217 when he shot down a Lancaster on 16 July 1943. By the end of that month, 235ª *Squadriglia* reported that six of its Dorniers were unserviceable and, due to a lack of spares, the last known sortie was flown on 16 August 1943. The unit subsequently converted to the Re.2001 single-seat fighter. This aircraft belly-landed at Lonate Pozzolo in late July or early August 1943 while being flown by Capt Ammanato, who later reported that he could not lower the undercarriage due to the presence of metallic fragments in the landing gear's hydraulic system. The unit badge, a lion with the inscription '*Nec in Somno Quies*' ('Even in sleep, rest'), adorned both sides of the Do 217's nose.

18
Do 217M-1 Wk-Nr 722852 U5+ET of 9./KG 2, Dreux, France, August 1943

Two Do 217M-1s with this code were lost during the summer of 1943. Wk-Nr 722852, flown by Leutnant Theo Bach, failed to return from a raid on Portsmouth on the night of 15–16 August. Caught in a searchlight beam, the pilot took violent evasive action that resulted in the aircraft hitting the ground and disintegrating at Broadway Farm, near Lovedean in Hampshire, at 0010 hrs, killing all four crew, of which only one, flight engineer Obergefreiter Werner Neubert, was buried. The camouflage pattern depicted here is how it was described by RAF intelligence officers who inspected the wreckage. The second U5+ET to be lost was Wk-Nr 56162, shot down off Ramsgate on the night of 15 September by Flg Off Ron Watts of No 488 Sqn. Oberfeldwebel Erich Möseler and his crew were all killed.

19
Do 217M-1 Wk-Nr 56125 U5+UK of 2./KG 2, Eindhoven, the Netherlands, September 1943

This aircraft suffered an accident at Eindhoven on 7 September 1943, incurring 15 per cent damage. It has the twin bands on the tail and the numeral on the rudder peculiar to I./KG 2, the reasoning behind these markings having never been fully explained. Repaired, Wk-Nr 56125 appears to have been given to 9./KG 2 and allotted the code U5+CT. The aircraft crashed into the North Sea following an attack on Hull on 20–21 April 1944, Obergefreiter Hermann Went and his crew (who were all lost) having almost certainly been shot down by Flg Off Harry White of No 141 Sqn. Note the last three digits of the Werknummer on the nose of the bomber.

20
Do 217E-5 Wk-Nr 5654 6N+NP of 6./KG 100, Istres, France, September 1943

The Do 217E-5, with its distinctive bulge beneath the nose glazing housing the control mechanism for the Hs 293, served operationally with II./KG 100. The unit suffered its first combat losses over Salerno on the night of 12–13 September 1943 when this aircraft and Wk-Nr 5555 were shot down. Wk-Nr 5654 was flown by Unteroffizier Willy Otto, and it was probably downed by Beaufighters of No 600 Sqn, which claimed six bombers destroyed. Three crew were reported missing and gunner Unteroffizier Othmar Springinsfeld returned. Although the Do 217E-5 could be armed with two Hs 293s, typically only one glide-bomb would be carried on the starboard side and a fuel tank fitted to the port side for added range. As the observer sat on the starboard side of the cockpit, this gave him a better view when it came to the difficult task of steering the bomb towards its target.

21
Do 217E-4 Z6+DH of 1./KG 66, Montdidier, France, September 1943

In April 1943, 1./KG 66 was formed at Chartres from 15./KG 6, which itself had been formed from *Lehr-und Erprobungskommando* 17. The latter's origins go further to *Lehr-und Erprobungskommando* 100, also known as *Erprobungskommando XY*. Its purpose was pathfinding – a role that the Ju 88 and Ju 188 were soon found to be better at than the Do 217, resulting in the Dornier being phased out by March 1944. Prior to then, 1./KG 66 had flown a mix of Do 217E-4s and K-1s equipped with Y Verfahren VHF single beam/range-measuring precision bombing equipment – hence the large FuG 28A aerial above the cockpit. The *Staffel* suffered its first combat loss before it had been declared fully operational when, at 0040 hrs on 21 June 1943, Unteroffizier Kurt Winter's Do 217K-1 Wk-Nr 4462 3E+AZ was probably shot down by Flt Lt Massy Beveridge of No 418 Sqn at Saint-Georges-du-Mesnil, near Montdidier. It is believed that the *Staffel's* 3E code (referring to its time as 15./KG 6) was changed to Z6 at the end of August 1943. Note the FuG 212 rear-warning receiver aerials beneath Z6+DH's wingtips.

22
Do 217J-1 G3+PV of 6./NJG 101, Lechfeld, Germany, autumn 1943

II./NJG 101, commanded by Major Hans-Dietrich Knoetzsch, was formed from II./*Nachtjagdschule* 1 at München-Riem at the end of March 1943. The *Gruppe* initially flew a mixed fleet of Bf 110s and Do 217J-1s, but it became increasingly a Dornier *Gruppe* – especially with the arrival of the N-1 from October – as 1943 progressed. Despite being a training unit, II./NJG 101 was also committed to frontline operations, suffering a number of losses as a result. Note that 6. *Staffel* used the letter V in its code, while 5. *Staffel* used T. This aircraft has had its radar aerials removed, which would indicate that its primary function was to serve as a crew trainer. Note also the *Nachtjagd* diving eagle insignia on the nose.

23
Do 217M-1 Wk-Nr 722851 U5+HS of 8./KG 2, Rennes, France, November 1943

Wk-Nr 722851 was apparently the personal aircraft of the *Staffelkapitän* of 8./KG 2, Oberleutnant Josef Steudel, and it was photographed flying from Eindhoven at the end of September 1943 during a formation training flight. All the Do 217s seen in shots from this period are similarly camouflaged. The aircraft was lost in an attack on Plymouth on the night of 15–16 November 1943 while being flown by Leutnant Klaus Dicke from Rennes, rather than from III./KG 2's home airfield at Eindhoven. Its demise was not caused by the RAF, who filed no claims that night, and the aircraft is assumed to have crashed in the Channel for Dicke and his crew were listed as missing.

24
Do 217K-3 Wk-Nr 4716 6N+IT of 9./KG 100, Toulouse-Francazal, France, April 1944

On the night of 29 April 1944, this aircraft was one of a number briefed to attack warships in Plymouth with '*Fritz X*' guided bombs. Flown by Leutnant Herbert Palme, Wk-Nr 4716 was shot down by a Mosquito from No 406 Sqn and crashed near Totnes, with Palme and two crew captured and one killed. RAF intelligence noted that this was the first time they had been able to examine the wreckage of a K-3, stating it had a wingspan of 80 ft 6 in. The fuselage code was all-black apart from a yellow letter I, its *Stammkennzeichen* was RO+YD and the undersurfaces were 'sky blue and the fuselage and top surfaces a very light blue, with green wavy lines superimposed'.

25
Do 217K-3 Wk-Nr 4749 6N+HR of 9./KG 100, Toulouse-Francazal, France, May 1944

Very few photographs exist of the Do 217K-3, and the first recorded accident involving this variant occurred on 20 October 1943, with another example (from 5./KG 100) being destroyed in an air attack on Kalamaki on 15 November 1943. The first combat loss of a K-3 occurred on 30 April 1944. Initially, a few K-3s served with 5./KG 100, although the major operating unit was III./KG 100. On the night of 14 June 1944, six aircraft, including this one flown by Feldwebel Rudolf Stoll, attacked warships in the Baie de Seine. During its return flight to Toulouse-Francazal, the aircraft (along with Do 217K-2 Wk-Nr 4555 6N+IT) flew into the ground near Saint-Laurent-de-Neste, 53 km east of Tarbes in southern France.

Oberfeldwebel Kurt Faust and his crew were killed, as were the crew of Wk-Nr 4555. The aircraft crashed in such a remote location that most of the wreckage was not recovered – much of one aircraft was thrown into a cave. By the time of its demise, Wk-Nr 4749 had be re-camouflaged similar to the aircraft seen in Profile 24. Despite having a 7./KG 100 code, this aircraft was recorded as operating with 9. *Staffel*.

26
Do 217N-1 Wk-Nr 1570 3C+IP of 6./NJG 6, Tavaux, France, May 1944

This aircraft, crewed by Feldwebel Günther Konzac (pilot), Unteroffizier Arthur Ruprecht (radio operator) and Obergefreiter Alfred Elster (gunner), became lost on a training sortie on 2 May 1944 and landed at Basel-Birsfelden in Switzerland, where the crew and aircraft were interned. Wk-Nr 1570, fitted with *Schräge Musik* cannon in the upper fuselage behind the cockpit, was never returned to Germany, the aircraft being repainted in Swiss air force markings and eventually scrapped. Note the FuG 202 Lichtenstein aerials protruding from the nose.

27
Do 217M-1 Wk-Nr 56347 K7+LH of 1./*Nachtaufklärungsstaffel*, Copenhagen, Denmark, May 1945

At the start of May 1945, the surviving *Nachtaufklärungsstaffeln* were told to disperse to airfields across Europe. This aircraft from Hauptmann Wilfried Petersen's 1./*Nachtaufklärungsstaffel* was captured at Copenhagen, the Dornier being painted in standard camouflage for *Nachtaufklärungsstaffeln*. Photographs of the Do 217 taken shortly after VE Day indicate that the LH section of the aircraft's code was applied in yellow (indicating its assignment to 3. *Staffel*, despite the latter having been disbanded in May 1944 and reformed as 1.(F)/123), with an identical shade of paint adorning the engines' lower cowlings. Note also that the swastika on the fin has been overpainted, but the last four digits of the Werknummer remain untouched. Wk-Nr 56347's previous history is not known, and it has been suggested that many aircraft came to the *Nachtaufklärungsstaffeln* from KG 2, which had been disbanded on 3 October 1944.

28
Do 217M-1 K7+AH of 1./*Nachtaufklärungsstaffel*, Linz-Hörsching, Austria, May 1945

Although sporting entirely different camouflage to K7+LH captured in Copenhagen, this aircraft does have the yellow cowlings beneath the engines and spiral spinners – the latter marking was adopted by many *Nachtaufklärungsstaffeln*. However, problems with cracks around the bolts also meant that a number of aircraft flew without spinners. Note the Do 217's prominent underwing crosses and its all-white fuselage codes. Following its capture, this aircraft, which became a popular local 'attraction' for occupying troops, never flew again and was scrapped in situ.

29
Do 217M-1 K7+EK of 2./*Nachtaufklärungsstaffel*, Prague Ruzyně, Czechoslovakia, May 1945

The diversity of camouflage for the *Nachtaufklärungsstaffeln* Do 217M-1s could indicate that they were aircraft handed over by other units. This Dornier was captured in a flyable condition at

Prague Ruzyně, and its ultimate fate is not known. Photographs have not emerged of K7+EK, although it was described as being 'camouflaged distempered back overall, with snaking grey mottling'. The aircraft had black cowlings beneath the engines and all-black propeller spinners. Do 217M-1 Wk-Nr 56527 K7+HK was also captured intact in May 1945, but at Beldringe, near Odense in Denmark, after which it was flown to the RAE at Farnborough, in Hampshire. It was seen on display at the latter site towards the end of the 1945, having been given the code AIR MIN 106. The aircraft was put into storage in 1946 and eventually scrapped in the mid-1950s.

30
Do 217M-1 Wk-Nr 56158 of RAE Farnborough, England, November 1945

This aircraft was one of six listed by the 2nd Tactical Air Force as captured at Odense in May 1945 in flyable condition. A further

Do 217 was unserviceable and used as a source for spare parts to support the flyers. All were stated as being part of 2./*Nachtaufklärungsstaffel*, this unit, commanded by Hauptmann Heinrich Engelhardt, being one of the very few still flying the Do 217 operationally at war's end. This aircraft's markings were overpainted with RAF roundels and code lettering AIR MIN 107. Note the last three digits of the Werknummer at the top of the tail and the last four digits crudely applied over the Swastika. It also had the letter L stencilled on midway down the rudder, which could indicate that the aircraft's full code was, at some stage, K7+LK. The Do 217 was flown to Schleswig, in northern Germany, at the end of August 1945 and then on to RAE Farnborough, where full handling trials were carried out two months later. It was then one of a number of captured aircraft put on display at the Exhibition of German Aircraft and Equipment held at Farnborough in October-November 1945, after which the Dornier was placed in storage and later scrapped.

Do 217E-2 Wk-Nr 1138 RH+EL has its engines tested prior to being handed over to the Luftwaffe. The aircraft also has the last two digits of the Werknummer repeated on both the fuselage cross and nose. Upgraded into an E-4, Wk-Nr 1138 was damaged in an accident at Salon-de-Provence, in southern France, on 18 April 1943 while serving with II./KG 101

INDEX